Creative Dating

Doug Fields
&
Todd Temple

Illustrations by Steve Björkman

OLIVER
NELSON

A Division of Thomas Nelson Publishers
Nashville • Atlanta • Camden • New York

Second printing

Published in Nashville, Tennessee, by Oliver-Nelson Books, a division of
Thomas Nelson, Inc., Publishers, and distributed in Canada by Lawson
Falle, Ltd., Cambridge, Ontario.

Printed in the United States of America.

Library of Congress Cataloging-in-Publication Data

Fields, Doug, 1962-
    Creative dating.

    1. Dating (Social customs)—Anecdotes, facetiae,
satire, etc.   I. Temple, Todd, 1958-   II. Title.
PN6231.D3F54   1986   818'.5402   86-5126
ISBN 0-8407-9541-6

To our wives,
Cathy and Katie,
whose love inspired our creativity
and whose belief allowed us to fulfill
one of our dreams.
We love you.

YOUR DATE IDEA COULD BE WORTH $500

Do you have a good date idea that you would like to share with others? Send your brainstorm to us. If we publish it in a future book we will send you $10.00 and print your name with your contribution. If we select yours as the most creative idea in the book, you will get a check for $500.00!

Don't keep your creative date to yourself. Write it down and send it to us with this form. Be sure to explain the idea as clearly as possible.

FILL OUT:

NAME _____

ADDRESS _____

CITY_____ STATE_____ ZIP_____

I hereby submit the attached dating idea(s) for possible publication in a future book on creative dating, attesting that to my knowledge the publication of these ideas by the authors of Creative Dating does not violate any copyright belonging to another party. I also understand that I will receive payment for these ideas if published by the authors, the amount to be determined by the authors, payable upon publication.

SIGNATURE_____ DATE_____

Write out or type your dating idea(s) and attach it to this form. Put your name somewhere on the idea(s) as well. Submitted material cannot be returned. Send to:

CREATIVE DATING
P.O. BOX 8329
NEWPORT BEACH, CA 92658–8329

Contents

Introduction

A date with someone special can be one of the most thrilling and memorable experiences of your life. The potential for romance, laughter, excitement, closeness, growth, communication and just plain fun is great in this delightful human ritual called dating. And yet, most people put surprisingly little effort into planning a date that is conducive to these wonderful possibilities. In this book, we present innovative ideas and practical principles you can use to create quite extraordinary dates and to encourage fun and fulfilling relationships.

This book is written for anyone who enjoys dating, including teenagers who are beginning to develop dating standards and habits; singles who enjoy dating but are eager for new ideas to spark their creativity; and married couples who want to rekindle the excitement of their courtship. (Who said that spouses should not date each other?)

Whatever your reasons for desiring to create special dates, we hope that you will find this book to be helpful in four ways. First, whether you read it cover to cover or skim through it to help you plan tonight's date, we hope that you can actually *use* some of the ideas.

Second, we want to *inspire* you to experience the best that a good dating relationship can offer and to use your own creativity to express the importance you place in the friendship.

Third, some people take dating too seriously and in so doing make themselves—and their dates—miserable during the entire experience. Laughing at our dating ideas now will help you to *laugh* at your own later on, when your most romantic plans go awry.

Finally, dating is just one of the countless simple joys we are free to share. We hope this book instills a genuine enthusiasm for dating and that you *communicate* that enthusiasm to others.

Read and enjoy,

Doug Fields & Todd Temple

1.

Cheap Dates

We believe that creativity, not money, is the essence of a great date. This chapter capitalizes on this belief. If you do not have—or do not wish to spend—lots of money, these dates will fit your budget. These dating ideas, along with the rest of the dates in this book, are just that—ideas. Use them to spur your own creativity as you design dates with a personal touch.

People Zoo

Take your date to the local zoo and be prepared to photograph a number of delightful creatures. Rather

than shoot animals on this safari, photograph the most incredible species at the zoo—the humans who visit it. Your goal is to capture on film the bizarre and comical behavior of the people who attempt to imitate the animals they are observing. Be aware of the following masterpieces:

- Human scratching under arm in front of monkey cage
- Person standing on one leg while checking out the flamingos
- Individual sticking out tongue at a snake
- Adult rolling in mud next to pig sty

If you cannot afford film, do not despair. With or without film, one of the best parts of the day is seeing your subjects' expressions when they hear your shutter click.

Puddle Jumping

Rather than let a rainstorm drown your fun, use it to create a splashy date. During the downpour, take your date for a walk through the streets, seeking puddles of water to play in. You can do many things with a water puddle. Have a splash war, splash for distance and height, or try to splash out all the water. Stand on a street corner and wait for cars and buses to douse you as they dash through the flooded intersection. For more fun let the driver think you were caught unaware; fall down and send the culprit away with a great laugh.

If there is a playground nearby, take advantage of the slide, which, in addition to being very slippery, is bound to have a juicy puddle at the bottom to cushion your landings. For more adventurous thrill seekers, get a flexible, plastic toboggan and try your luck on a wet, grassy hill. When you return from your puddle-jumping excursion, recuperate in front of the fireplace with some hot liquid refreshment.

On to the Sales

On any given weekend, a quick glance through the classified section can lead you and your date to a number of garage sales and open houses. There are many fun things to do at a garage sale. For instance, find the most ridiculous polyester knit outfit on the clothes rack, and ask if you can try it on; bring some of your own junk, and leave it there on consignment; ask how much they want for their garage; make some money by selling cookies and lemonade from a stand in front of the house (with permission, of course!).

When looking at other people's junk gets tiring and

you are actually beginning to like the double knits, it is time to follow the signs to an open house. Do not go to just any open house. Find the largest, most expensive estate on the market. While touring the house be sure to do the things that home shoppers do: try the faucets, flush the toilets, check for dust on the tops of doors, and handle everything. For added enjoyment, dress the part, talk interest rates, and be sure to mention "the Club" at least twice.

Up on the Roof

Start the day with your date in an unusual way. Find a way up to the roof just before sunrise. If there is a flat section, bring lawn chairs and a hot drink. If both of you are "morning people," bring a tape player and waltz in the new day as the sun peers over the horizon. Climb back up at sunset to watch the day end.

People Watching

Airports, bus stations, shopping malls, and college campuses are prime locations for partaking in this skilled art. Find a comfortable spot and begin to observe the crowd. First, try to guess where people are from, their destination, occupation, and the type of

car or pet they own. Next, play "I See So-and-So." Look around and find a person who reminds you of a famous person or a mutual friend. Without pointing out the look-alike, say, "I see . . ." and then name the person who resembles someone in view. Your date now must discreetly point out the look-alike. Now switch roles and try to find someone your date picks out.

When you have seen enough famous personalities for one day, go eat some ice cream. The most exciting thing about people watching is noticing the immense variety and the wonderful uniqueness displayed by the Creator in each individual.

Cheap Food

Visit local restaurants to discover where you can eat the most food for the least money. At a seafood place,

order a bowl of clam chowder and two spoons. Ask for an extra bag of oyster crackers, and see if bread comes with the meal. At a Mexican restaurant, fill up on chips and dip; then order a plate of refried beans with cheese melted on top, and a few hot tortillas. Roll the beans and cheese into the tortilla to make a burrito. Be sure to split your savings with your waiter or waitress by giving them a large tip.

Green Thumb

Go to the nursery and buy some packets of seeds. Ask neighbors for additional seeds and plant cuttings. Start your own garden in a yard or window box. Maintain the garden together. (If the entire garden dies, break up!)

Discount Seats

Although concerts can be very entertaining, they can also be very expensive. A fine way to enjoy a concert without shelling out lots of money is to sit *outside* the concert hall or amphitheater. Many concerts, especially those held outdoors, can be heard (and occasionally seen) quite well from the parking lot or from behind the stage doors. Bring a couple of lawn chairs, and make yourselves comfortable in a spot where the sound is best. If the concert features a lively rock band, the sound will easily escape the confines of the hall. An added bonus is that the gates are often opened during the last several minutes of a concert to facilitate exiting; you then have the opportunity to see the final songs and to satisfy your desire to get a glimpse of the performers. This date is also ideal if crowds make you nervous or if high sound levels are uncomfortable for you.

Do not be surprised if the "discount spots" are

nearly taken by the time you arrive. Many people prefer this experience to paying for a ticket only to have their ears damaged and their view blocked by the back of someone's head during the entire concert.

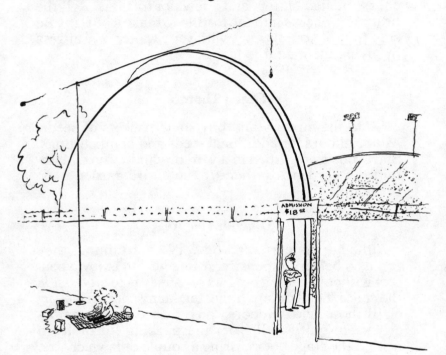

Library Mania

Often the word *library* is associated with other words like *boring, quiet, academic,* and *fines.* Very seldom is it associated with anything exciting. This may sound crazy, but there are some incredibly fun things to do in the library. Because every library is different, you may be able to use only a few of the following ideas:

- Visit the *children's section* and read some of the stories as you sit in the very small chairs. Some children's books are brilliantly written and communicate simple messages that are good to hear.
- View movies. If the library has a *movie room*, it will usually have a fair supply of 16mm movies that can be viewed right there or taken home. Check the film catalog for a favorite, or be daring and try a title that you have never heard of.
- Search through the *card catalog* or computer file for an author with the same full name as yours.
- Play "Musical Phones." If the library has two *pay phones* next to each other, go to one phone and dial the number of the other phone. As it is ringing, pretend you are busy talking on your phone and cannot answer the ringing phone. When someone comes to answer the phone, disconnect yours with your hand but continue to talk into the handset.
- Find the room where the *old magazines and newspapers* are kept. Libraries usually have back issues of periodicals and newspapers. Find a magazine or newspaper dated on or near your birthday to see what things were like when you were born. Look for historical headlines in newspapers. Reading accounts of historic moments from old newspapers and magazines is much more exciting than reading a history book.
- Find *out-of-state phone books* and look for addresses and numbers of distant friends or family.
- Browse through the library's *record collection*. Try a different style of music in the listening room. Test your date's knowledge of music by naming a song title and then asking for the artist's or group's name.
- Check out a *"how to" book,* and go home to put it

to work. If the book happens to describe how to assemble a microwave oven using scrap metal and a transistor radio . . . make plans for another cheap date at a later time.

Romance in the Park

Have a traditional picnic with checkered cloth, wicker basket, and ants in the mustard. Do somersaults on the grass—see who can do the most without getting sick. Try mowing the grass . . . by hand. Pick up litter. Sit at opposite ends of a bench and pretend you don't know each other. Then, after a series of curious glances, move slowly toward each other until you grasp hands and gaze into each other's eyes. Look up to see if you have attracted a crowd.

THIS IS THE BEST! A WALK WITH YOU AND PUBLIC SERVICE AT THE SAME TIME!

Adult Education

Check your local college, recreation department, or newspaper community-events calendar for a listing of

upcoming, free classes and lectures. Instead of going to dinner and a movie, you and your date can see a slide show on "Butterflies of Madagascar," or hear lectures on "Cooking Without Food," "Tap Dancing for Infants," or "How to Build a Nuclear Submarine in Your Garage in Your Spare Time Using Common Hand Tools."

Rock Skipping

Head to the nearest beach, river, lake, pond, or bird-bath to partake in an age-old test of skill. Rock skipping is a very cheap date that can provide plenty of challenge and laughter. The goal is to hurl a stone so that it bounces upon the water's surface as many times as possible. After you have skipped all the good rocks on the shore (or thrown your arm out trying), give each other some well-deserved shoulder and arm massages, take a swim, soak your feet, or set adrift a piece of wood and bomb it with pebbles as it floats past. If you are near a river or stream, make boats out of bark and race them downstream.

Before you leave, secretly slip a few good skipping rocks into your pocket; in a few weeks you can leave them where your date will find them as a reminder of your time together.

Skipping Chart

0 skips	lousy date idea
1–4 skips	should practice before doing this date again
5–7 skips	average
8–12 skips	Olympic hopeful
13–15 skips	expert
16 or more	liar

Free Television

Staying at home to watch television can be a cheap date idea, unless for some reason you do not have a TV. If the program is too good to miss, pack a snack and take your date to the local hospital. The fathers'

lounge in the maternity section is sure to have a comfortable spot where the two of you can enjoy the show. Be sure to share your snacks with any expectant fathers. Who knows, you may leave with a cigar.

Free Food

Have your own scavenger lunch by visiting friends and neighbors to ask for handouts. At the first house, ask for two pieces of bread. At the next house, ask for a spread of peanut butter. Other houses can provide you with jam, a banana, a glass of milk, a carrot, and a cookie. The trick is that you can accept only one ingredient from each house. Share your well-earned meal.

If you are still hungry, visit supermarkets for free samples and taste tests. While wandering the market aisles, look for the grossest food on the shelves. The gourmet section usually has several potential winners. With your thumbnail, mark the label on a tube of anchovy paste or a jar of sturgeon eggs. Come back the following week to see if the marked item is still there. If it is missing, somebody probably bought it and could be spreading it on crackers and eating it at this very moment.

Anonymous Affirmation

Agree with your date on the name of a person whom you both respect, appreciate, or admire. This person could be a mutual friend, teacher, co-worker, or anyone you think is special. Make notes of some of the things you really like about him or her, then compose a letter telling the person your sincere feelings. Type the letter to ensure anonymity, or cut and paste a note with pictures and words from magazines. Mail the letter.

Cheap Culture

Weekly, many local newspapers list concerts, art shows, dance productions, plays, and other presentations that can be attended free of charge. For the cost of a paper, you and your date may be exposed to a new world of entertainment.

Tourist Dates

Many factories, companies, and organizations offer tours of their facilities at little or no cost. Taking one of these tours as a date activity can be an inexpensive and educational experience.

Places to Tour

airplane factory
alligator farm
barbed wire factory
book bindery
electrical generating
   station
glass manufacturer
hydroponic greenhouse
ice-cream factory
junk mail clearing
   house
mint
museum
newspaper pressroom

paper recycling factory
photo lab
radio station
shoe factory
soft drink bottling
   company
sound studio
stadium or sports arena
telephone company,
   operators' section
television station
tennis ball factory
wax museum
zoo

ALLIGATORS ARE BASICALLY HARMLESS... UNLESS YOU'RE AFRAID. IF THEY SENSE FEAR THEY'LL RIP YOU TO PIECES!

Back to Nature

Visit the library to check out books on geology, ecology, birds, or plants. Take your date to a park, wildlife refuge, or natural open space to test your knowledge. Try to identify various species in the wild, or trace the origin of some geologic formations.

Join a guided nature walk or bird-watching tour being conducted in the area. While on the tour, occasionally stare and point to imaginary wildlife and have your date play along. Take note of how many people the two of you succeed in tempting to take a look. Also, try to count the number of people who actually claim to see what you were pretending to point out.

For even more fun, dress in camouflage gear and hide in the bushes a stone's throw from the nature trail. As people walk along the trail, rustle the bushes and make low, growling noises. Carefully peek to see if you have gathered a crowd (beware of binoculars). If someone leaves the trail to get a closer look, snarl loudly. If this fails to turn the scout around and you are discovered, look up and say "Shhh! You've scared the bear cub away. We have been hiding here to observe its behavior."

When acting like animals gets boring, find a remote meadow. Practice ballroom dancing to the sound of the bird and cricket orchestra. Have a picnic on the edge of a creek. Afterward, lie back and stare at the clouds. Visualize familiar objects or persons in the shapes of the clouds.

Visit different areas during the various seasons to experience the many moods of these natural playgrounds.

Stroll in Style

Visit a thrift store together and purchase matching, outlandish outfits, preferably from the same era.

Stroll through your town (or someone else's if you are worried about your images), basking in the attention of passers-by. Hats, canes, umbrellas, wigs, glasses, jewelry, and purses can put the finishing touches on your costumes.

Cheap Labor

Find an elderly person in the neighborhood who needs some yardwork, painting, or cleanup done, and

spend the day working for free. (Working with people is one of the best ways to learn what they are really like.) If the recipient of the free labor offers you money, refuse. If the person insists by stapling the money to your shirt, treat yourselves to a milk shake, then give the rest of the money to an organization that ministers to the needs of the elderly.

Here are some other worthwhile ideas you can try:

- Visit a nursing home
- Volunteer in a hospital
- Volunteer at a church
- Take disabled children on a ride
- Do dishes at a rescue mission
- Enter a jog-a-thon for a worthy cause

(We strongly recommend this activity but suggest you avoid it on a first date.)

Sunset Show

Rather than pay several dollars for a movie at the theater, get a front row seat to view one of God's most spectacular productions, the sunset. You are welcome to add some nice music and a picnic dinner. This awesome show appears daily; be looking for the best location near you.

Bicycling for Two

Go for a bicycle ride in a park or rural area where you can ride without fear of being run over. Instead of

riding quickly for miles to get to a specific place, take your time and play some of these bike games along the way:

- *Slow Races:* Without steering off a narrow path or putting a foot down, see how much time it takes each of you to travel a distance of twenty feet.
- *Precision Riding:* On a street with no traffic, practice weaving in and out of each other's paths in a finely orchestrated pattern. Bring a small radio and set your "bicycle ballet" to music.
- *Coasting Race:* With one shove at the top of a hill, see how far each of you can travel without pedaling before having to put a foot down.
- *Little Kids' Bikes:* Put streamers in the ends of the handlebars. Make engine sounds by sticking a playing card into the spokes with a clothespin attached to the forks.
- *Follow the Leader:* Steer a difficult course and see how long your date can keep up.

When all of this playful riding has tired you out, take a rest in the shade of a tree. Enjoy some fruit and cold drinks from a backpack before turning homeward.

Seeing Stars

Skim through a book on astronomy from the library to learn the names and positions of some of the stars, constellations, and planets visible in the night sky. Invite your date to a late-night astronomy lesson, and go to a clear place where you can sit back comfortably and watch the stars. Try to locate the celestial objects you have studied, and take turns creating new constellations. Watch for shooting stars and satellites. Make up stories about UFOs and see whose tale is more believable.

Run for Your Money

Take fifteen dimes, twenty nickels, and forty-eight pennies (which comes to $2.98), and spread them out on the pavement in front of a theater one minute before a little kids' matinee lets out. You and your date should each estimate how long it will take for the side-

walk to be picked clean. Start the clock when the first kid discovers the treasure, and stop it when all the coins are gone. Whoever guesses closest to the actual time wins and gets treated to a root beer float.

Go Fly a Kite

Make your own kites (look in the library for ideas) and fly them in an open field. Have a dogfight with them. See which one will fly the highest. Thread bathroom tissue cores on the string, and let the wind blow them up to the kites. See how many cores you can run up the string without crashing the kites. Carefully land your kites and save them for another day.

Stickbread in the Park

Take your date to a beach, park, or other open area where you can safely build a fire. Be sure to bring all the items on the checklist. After getting a small fire going (this may be the toughest part), start mixing up some dough using the directions on the box. Roll a small handful of dough into a ball, then pound it into a thick pancake. Wrap the dough around a stick, and let it bake over the fire. When the bread has risen sufficiently and has turned golden brown, peel it off the stick, add butter, honey, jam, or whatever, and eat. For dessert you can cook some marshmallows on a coat hanger and sandwich them between graham crackers and chocolate bars. Bring some milk to wash it all down.

Checklist

☐ kindling
☐ firewood
☐ two sticks (one inch diameter, three feet long)
☐ matches

☐ box of Bisquick or other baking mix
☐ mixing bowl
☐ water
☐ spoon
☐ butter, jam, honey, or whatever
☐ marshmallows
☐ graham crackers
☐ chocolate bars
☐ coat hanger
☐ milk

Johnny Carson and Chicken Noodle Soup

If you are going to watch television on a date, at least do it creatively. Find a portable TV and take it, along with your date and some hot chicken noodle soup (*Poultry Digest* reports that "chicken is the most romantic member of the fowl family") to the beach, park, or other secluded spot with clear reception. Tune in Johnny Carson, and enjoy the show from your spacious "living room."

Hot Tub and Cider

Grab a bottle of sparkling cider and take your date to a nearby hot tub. Rather than just soak until your bodies resemble prunes, try these tub games:

- *Whirlpool:* The two of you walk in a circle for a couple of minutes until the entire pool is swirling. Take turns jumping into the center to ride the liquid twister.

- *Jet Plug:* If the pool has air jets, see how many you can plug up with your body.

- *Freshwater Whale:* Jump into the water without touching the bottom or the sides when you hit. In most tubs this feat can only be accomplished with a backflop. If you succeed, consider yourself a winner—and an idiot for taking this game seriously.

To avoid embarrassment on a hot tub date, be aware of the following facts:

- Not everyone looks great in a bathing suit; your date may not want to be seen, or to see you, in a suit.
- If you lie back on the deck with your feet in the tub, your wet back may make a loud sound when you sit up.
- If you soak too long, your prune-textured body may end a relationship based too heavily on physical appearances.

Kiss Avoidance Procedures

Kissing is incredible—when experienced with the right person. In case you do not happen to be with that person when about to be kissed, try one of these tactics:

What to Say

- My lips are really sunburned.
- I'm feeling sick all of a sudden.
- I just had my braces tightened.
- The last time I kissed, I bit my partner's lips off.
- Have you ever met my boyfriend? He is the bouncer at Jake's Dance Hall.
- I am a pilgrim (Puritan).

- These really are not my lips.
- I have mononucleosis.
- My parents are watching.
- It is amazing how I can still taste the anchovy pizza I ate three hours ago.

What to Do

- Give yourself a nose bleed.
- Clear your throat.
- Stick a plug of chewing tobacco in your mouth.
- Blow a chewing gum bubble in the person's face.
- Have a runny nose.
- Put garlic in your mouth and cough.
- Flip your retainer or dentures in and out of your mouth.
- Put on a plastic nose and glasses.
- Put pepperoni in your teeth.

Saying Goodnight at the Doorstep

- Tell a story that wears the person down so he or she will want to leave.
- Accidentally lean up against the door bell, causing your parents or roommates to answer the door.
- Wear his jacket so he will get cold waiting at the door.
- Let your dog out and give it a big slobbery kiss.

Constructive Dating

If you and your date happen to be feeling ambitious, build something. If there's snow on the ground, try to build an igloo. If you can find a beach, build a sand

castle. If the weather is bad, borrow a little kid's construction-block collection and build a mansion or skyscraper.

Little League

Throughout the year, boys' and girls' sports leagues battle it out on fields, courts, and rinks across the country. Grab some lounge chairs and sodas, and plant yourselves on the sideline of one of these events. You and your date will find that watching a pack of eight-year-olds you have never met before can be quite entertaining. If the action gets dull, turn your chairs around and watch the parents, who burn more calories cheering than the kids do playing. If things get re-

ally slow, stand near the snack bar and watch the two
volunteer mothers frantically attempt to serve thirty-
seven chili dogs to the team of impatient first graders
whose game is next.

2.

Moderate Dates

For the times when you have a bit more money, these dates are designed to give you the most delight for your dollar. If you are going to spend the cash, you might as well get your money's worth.

U-Haul Your Date

A large U-Haul truck can be the site of a truly "moving" date. Rent a U-Haul truck or some other large

moving van, and fill it with furniture. A couch, plants, dining table, soft music, and candles will provide a comfortable atmosphere.

Pick up your date and drive to a spot where you can watch the sunset from your "living room." Invite a violinist to rehearse in a nearby car. Visit a drive-in restaurant with carhops and have them serve you in the back of the truck. Park in the last row of a drive-in theater; pretend that you are watching a big-screen television in your den.

If you think this idea is too much work for one date, rent the furnished truck to a friend for the following night.

Dinghy With Crew

If you have seen romantic pictures of couples nestled together in a gondola being poled through the canals of Venice, you can image how wonderful this date can be. Take your special friend to a lake or harbor marina. Rent a small rowboat or canoe to act as your gondola, and recruit a friend to act as gondolier. Stack up life preservers or seat cushions to make a comfort-

MAKE SURE YOU ARE BETTER-LOOKING THAN YOUR GONDOLIER.

able backrest for you and your date, and stow on board any liquid refreshment you might want to serve while under way.

Allow your gondolier to give you a slow, peaceful tour upon the waterways while you concern yourself with your date's happiness. Let the boat drift freely for a few minutes so that you can hear the lapping of the water against the hull. If your cruise takes place in the evening, sit quietly in the boat and watch the reflections of lights dance and sparkle on the water's surface.

If after all this effort, your date does not seem to want to get into the romantic mood, throw your gondolier overboard—with a life preserver of course—and request that he or she swim ashore. After all, there is no one to blame but the gondolier.

Stadium Frolics

Take your date to any nearby stadium, and purchase the cheapest ticket. Instead of going to your cheap seats, see if you can somehow make your way to the more expensive seats. You will not want to stay there—just do it for the sake of a challenge. Now grab something to write on, and position yourselves in front of one of the aisles. Take a survey of the kind of food people purchase at the snack bar. Offer to give the person carrying the most food a hand in transporting the supplies back to his or her seat if you can have one bite or sip of each thing you carry.

Ask the person selling popcorn in the stands if it comes with mayonnaise. Try this with every popcorn vendor in the stadium so that when they all meet at the end of the day to check out and to share their "weirdo" stories, you and your date will be famous. After this, walk slowly in front of the stands and pretend you are looking for someone. You may even want to shout a name like John, Bob, or Mary to see how many people respond.

Ask a walking vendor for change for a five-hundred-dollar bill, a good price on season tickets, or a Susan B. Anthony dollar. Walk around until you find a group of ushers or police officers, and begin to pick up the stadium's litter. You may even precede the trash sweeper to make the person's job easier. Make sure you run up and down the stadium ramps in bizarre ways. Finally, go to your original seats and watch the remainder of the game. Cheer with great enthusiasm for one team, and then switch after a few minutes.

Does this sound like a winner, sports fans?

Buried Treasure

Make a pirate's treasure map out of parchment paper, giving directions to a treasure you have buried somewhere in your area. In case you have never seen a real pirate's treasure map, it generally features a skull and crossbones, lines of dashes representing paces from nearby trees or rocks, and an *X* at the location of the treasure. Also, the edges look as if they have been set on fire.

Before making the map of course, you will need to locate a site to bury the treasure. Pick a sandy spot that is easy to dig. Just before you meet your date, dis-

creetly bury your treasure. You can bury an entire picnic lunch in a box or plastic trash bag, or you can
simply bury a small gift. If you and your date fail to
find the treasure you have buried, then you know other
pirates watched you bury it and came back for the
booty.

Dinner to Go

If the evening plans call for a long drive to a concert,
play, or other performance, break up the monotony of
the drive by serving a romantic, light meal en route.

Rig up a small tray to set your meal on between the

front seats. Lay down a small, white tablecloth and
two cloth napkins. Pull a bottle of sparkling red grape
juice from an ice bucket in the back seat, and serve in
crystal tumblers (or, if you're really brave, crystal gob-
lets!). Set out a large plate of sliced cheeses, meats,
breads, crackers, vegetables, and fruits.

For atmosphere, include on the tray a small,
weighted vase containing a rose. Since a candle would
be unwise in this setting, try this safe alternative.
Place a waterproof, pocket-size flashlight in a watertight jar filled with water. For effect, you can color the
water with food coloring. The soft colorful glow of the
water-lamp will provide ample illumination without
making it difficult to see through the windows.

When the meal is over, reach into a small cooler in the back seat to remove two ice-cream bars for dessert. Eating dinner on the road in this fashion can turn an otherwise tiring drive into a memorable adventure.

Taking Lessons

A great way to learn a new skill is by taking lessons along with a special friend. Having someone learn with you makes the lessons more enjoyable and gives the two of you a regularly scheduled time to be together.

Sign up together to learn how to play golf, tennis, bridge, or the French horn; or take a computer, sculpturing, or cooking class as a couple. Being together can make even the tough parts enjoyable, and the time spent together practicing, studying, and learning will teach you much about each other. A WORD OF CAUTION: If the teacher sees too much promise in your date's abilities and offers free private lessons—without you—it is time for the two of you to drop the class.

Cloning Around

This unique date takes time, ingenuity, and a great deal of patience and self-control. Before the date begins, spend some time recording a cassette tape. The voice on this tape will be that of a secret service agent (played by a friend, or by you with an altered voice); go to your local library, and borrow a sound effects

record to make the tape more realistic. On the completed tape, the agent will inform your date that you have been kidnapped for use in a top-secret project and that a clone has been constructed to take your place for the day. (Obviously this clone will be played by you.) The tape will also inform your date that it is of the utmost importance that he or she carefully follow the detailed instructions so as not to reveal to anyone that you are missing.

Now your patience and self-control are needed. At the beginning of the tape, make sure the secret service agent tells your date that the clone cannot speak and that he or she will have to rely completely on the taped instructions. If anyone asks the clone a question, your date will have to answer for you. Make sure your taped instructions on the day's activities are clear enough so that your date will be able to follow them without asking you any questions. Before recording the tape, be certain that the whole day's activities are clearly planned. Remember that your nonspeaking clone cannot change things once the day has begun. Bring in friends or family who know what is going on to be part of the fun.

When the date is over, the clone should leave; the "real you" can return the next day or a few hours later, not remembering anything. Make your date explain the whole day as if you really were not there.

ONE IMPORTANT HINT: Make sure he or she does not like the nonspeaking clone better than you.

Greens Touring

At many public golf courses, it is possible to drive or walk the course without being required to actually play it. You may be expected to pay cart rental and greens fees, but it is well worth the price if the course is especially well designed and maintained. Being the first ones out or the last ones in will help ensure that you are all by yourselves.

Free Swinging

Remember elementary school when there was a mad dash to be the first to the swings when the recess bell rang? You and your date can experience that same

excitement no matter what your ages. Instead of taking your date to just any swing set to swing, look for the perfect location to build your own; any big tree with strong branches is a potential swinging tree. If you want to add some risk to this new adventure, look for a tree next to water or one located where you can begin swinging from a hillside above the base of the tree.

Once the location is determined, go to a hardware store and buy the necessary materials. Set up your swing and take it for a test ride. If all is safe, take turns swinging, and attempt some double riding. (If you wish to leave the swing hanging but would like to keep others from hurting themselves on it, build a swing like the one shown in the illustration.) Once the swing is installed, you have a cheap date at your disposal anytime you and your date are in the mood for swinging—and you do not even need to wait for the recess bell.

Handouts

This date is a very quick way to spend a moderate amount of money. As you and your date are walking down the street on your way to a restaurant, take turns handing crisp one-dollar bills to passers-by. The expressions on the faces of the bewildered recipients will be highly entertaining—until your pockets are empty. If one of you walks several paces behind the other, the view is even better. When you have given away the last bill, stop and open your wallet. Pretend that you have mistakenly given away the twenty-dollar bill you had saved for dinner and that your date will have to pay for the meal. After the dinner check has been paid, "find" your money.

Dinner and a Movie

Although "dinner and a movie" is not exactly a creative date, there are ways to spice up this cultural norm in dating behavior. For example, plan on shopping for, preparing, and eating a special meal at home. Before you and your date go shopping, tie your inside hands and legs together. If someone stares at you and your date as you stroll the aisles, hand the person a copy of this book and continue shopping. The shopping experience will merely be a warm-up for the truly challenging task of preparing and eating your meal while tied together.

Instead of paying a lot of money to see a film that will be on television in several months, why not spend the remainder of your evening making your own movie? Borrow or rent a video camera and locate a set for filming. One person films and directs while the other plays the role of commentator. Interview people as they leave elevators, restaurants, and theaters. Explain that you are filming for a special television show (your own), and ask interviewees if they would like to smile and say hello to Mom. The commentator can ask

THIS IS DARLENE GLITZ
FOR CREATIVE DATE NEWS,
BACK TO YOU, CARL.....

questions like "Are the reports true that you intend to run for president?"; "Could you explain the universe and give three examples?"; or "After wasting good money to see this movie, how do you feel?"

Sports Dates

Here is a list of different sporting activities that you could try out on a date:

archery	diving
ATC riding	downhill skiing
badminton	driving range
basketball	exercise park
batting cage	fencing
bicycling	foursquare
billiards	frisbee
bodysurfing	golf
bowling	handball
boxing	high jumping
catch	hiking
croquet	horseback riding
cross-country skiing	jet skiing
curling	jogging
darts	jump rope

I GUESS I CAN TOO SHOOT PRETTY WELL "FOR A GIRL" AND I DON'T THINK I'LL BE HEARING YOU CALL ME "CAROL THE BARBARIAN" AGAIN WILL I ?

When you have shot enough footage—or bothered enough innocent people—head home and run your show. After an evening like this, you may never want to go on a "dinner and a movie" date again.

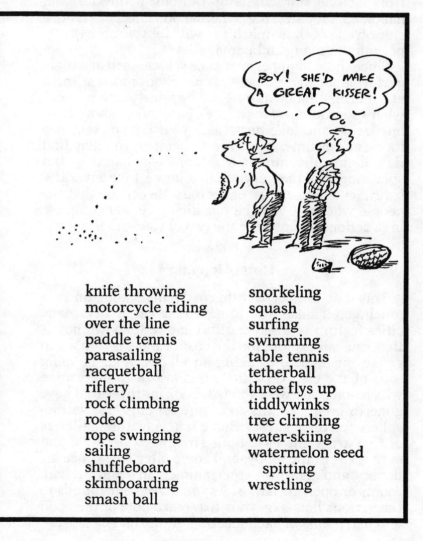

knife throwing
motorcycle riding
over the line
paddle tennis
parasailing
racquetball
riflery
rock climbing
rodeo
rope swinging
sailing
shuffleboard
skimboarding
smash ball

snorkeling
squash
surfing
swimming
table tennis
tetherball
three flys up
tiddlywinks
tree climbing
water-skiing
watermelon seed
  spitting
wrestling

Jet Ski

These jet-powered, aquatic vehicles are one of the most exciting high-tech toys on the market. The controls include start and stop buttons, a throttle, and handlebars for steering. Whether you kneel or stand, a ride on one of these machines will deliver more thrills per minute than can be imagined.

Since these high-performance vehicles sell at a high-performance price, many people choose to rent them at a marina that owns a fleet. The hourly rate is about what you would pay for a nice dinner and a show. Rent one jet ski and take turns with your date or rent two for a shorter time. If you are a beginner, you may find that about thirty minutes of bouncing, spinning, and splashing is all the fun you can tolerate. Like any water sport, jet skiing can be dangerous. Be certain that the people who rent you the machine give you complete instructions and provide the two of you with life vests.

Hotel-Hopping

This date may be a little costly, depending on how much gas it takes you to get into a large city. Many cities feature several beautiful and well-known hotels that you can explore for the cost of the gas it takes to get to them. Before taking an all-day, hotel-hopping tour of the city, do a little homework to determine which hotels are worth a visit. Look for those that have gone to great lengths to create an enjoyable atmosphere for their guests. Some hotels feature galleries of fine art; some have built streams, waterfalls, and even lakes in the lobby; and some offer free concerts, dances, and nighttime entertainment in beautiful ballrooms or open-air patios. As you make your rounds to the various hotels on your list, make note of the good and bad points of each location. At the end of the day, write a summary of the tour, and put together a regional guide to hotel-hopping for your friends.

Roadside Delivery

Imagine this scene: You and your date are casually sitting in lawn chairs in the grassy center island of a boulevard. Suddenly two egg salad sandwiches in a crash-proof container come whizzing past you from the open window of a speeding car, striking the ground just a few feet from where you are seated. You get up, grab the sandwiches, hand one to your date, and exclaim enthusiastically, "Oh boy! Here comes lunch!" In the next few minutes, you are deluged with more projectiles: various types of fruit, a carton of milk, a bag of potato chips, and a bag of cookies. Before lunch is over, a paperback book, two magazines, a frisbee, and a fifteen-piece croquet set land all around you.

This extremely bizarre and unforgettable date is made possible through the tireless efforts of friends who periodically drive past your location to throw you things to eat, drink, play, and do. Give these generous people a list of things you would like them to throw at

you and, of course, a map to where you will be waiting.

There are no rules to this date, except that you must be in the center or on the side of a pleasant road. You can try the experience at any time of the day for any length of time. Try a breakfast-and-morning-paper delivery or a sunset-with-hors-d'oeuvres delivery. The most important part to this date is that you thoroughly enjoy it. Your date may be concerned that you are capable of dreaming up such a bizarre pastime, but you will leave no doubt that you know how to enjoy yourself.

Elegance in Motion

Although not as popular as they once were, dance schools still give very enjoyable and effective lessons in ballroom dancing. Sign up for the generally discounted introductory lesson, and make a date out of it. The chances are great that you will enjoy the first lesson so much that you and your date will take a complete course. When the music is right at a dance, wedding, or banquet, the two of you will get the opportunity to show just how worthwhile this date was.

Romantic Dinner Spots

As you regularly travel throughout your community, make a point of looking for romantic spots you can use for future dates. Keep your eyes open for the following places:

- The secluded corner of a park
- A grassy hill
- A green pasture
- A deserted beach
- An old pier
- The roof of your office or apartment building

- A friend's balcony or patio
- Anything overlooking water

Select one of these sites for a dinner date. Rather than make the meal a picnic, coax, bribe, or pay a friend to act as caterer to your intimate party.

A sturdy cardboard box makes a fine table when covered with a tablecloth, and lawn chairs will seat you in style. The advantage of eating at one of these romantic spots is that you never have to wait for a table.

Slip 'n' Slide

If you have the right weather and location, this date is hard to top. Some toy stores still carry something popular a few years ago called a "Slip 'n' Slide." This long strip of wet plastic can be rolled out on a lawn or grassy hill and used as a slide. If you cannot find a real "Slip 'n' Slide," improvise with a thin sheet of plastic four feet wide and thirty feet long. Buy a length of plastic at a hardware store, or dig through the trash container behind a furniture store (the plastic is frequently used to wrap furniture for shipping). Lay the

YOU GO FIRST.

plastic on a hill, and find some way to keep it wet (hose, buckets of water, sprinklers) so that it will be easier to slide on. If the slide fails to cool you off sufficiently, run through the sprinklers, or have a water-balloon or squirt-gun fight. If you can handle being soaked by your date, try this idea on the next scorching-hot day.

Friend Masquerade

One way to make an evening more memorable is to have your friends play a part in it. Let them know the role they will be playing ahead of time so that they can act and play the part without breaking character.

Here is an idea that can include several friends. Pick up your date and drive her to your creative spot (see "Romantic Dinner Spots"). Have friend number one waiting to meet you there to valet park your car. As you enter your restaurant setting, your hostess (friend number two) will greet you and take you to your table. After you are seated at your table, the maitre d' (friend number three) will welcome you to this high-class restaurant, make sure you are comfortable, and tell you the restaurant's fictitious history. Next, your waiter (friend number four) will bring a calligraphic menu of the evening meal.

Once the meal is served, a fifth friend can enter, offering a rose to your date. Later in the meal, have a sixth friend enter dressed as a reporter from a local newspaper. As he takes numerous photographs, he can explain that he is doing a feature story on this establishment and wanted to photograph the most lovely (not to mention the only) couple in the restaurant. Of course an evening of this caliber requires a fine beverage. Arrange for a seventh friend to dress up in a mask, snorkel, bathing suit, and hiking boots. In his arms he will be carrying a bottle of wine or sparkling apple ci-

JUST PRETEND WE'RE ALL ALONE....

der. As he delivers the beverage, he can explain that he swam the imported drink into the country and hiked it to this restaurant especially for your date.

By taking the time and effort to include your friends in this special evening, you have made the evening more memorable for your date and demonstrated to your friends that they play an important part in your life.

Big City Sights

If you live in or near a large city, the chances are good that there are interesting sights frequented by out-of-towners that you as a local have never taken the time to see. By hiring a cab for an hour, you and your date can have a tour of the city by someone who knows it best. Bring a camera and be sure to dress as if you are from out of state. If the sights are less than exciting, you can still enjoy the ride by counting the number of near misses, horn honks, and lane changes your cabby makes in the time it takes the meter to run up another dollar. In this way you can calculate which mile gave you the most thrills for your money.

Musical Restaurants

Many restaurants are known for an exceptionally delicious item on their menu. Since different establishments are famous for different parts of a meal, it seems logical that you can have an extraordinary meal by hopping from one restaurant to the next for each course.

The first stop of the evening is a place famous for its appetizers. The next destination is the finest salad bar in the area. When you and your date are prepared for the main event, visit a restaurant known for its entrées. Finish off this moving meal at the spot with the finest desserts in the land. Afterward, you and your date will be able to look back on your evening and know that you had the finest combination of foods available in town.

Random Pictures

Before the actual date, take photographs of places you would like to go or things you would like to do on your date. For example, take photographs of a favorite restaurant, a whirlpool, a path you enjoy walking, a theater marquee, and a board game. After developing the film, place each of the prints in a separate envelope.

Let your date select and open any one of the envelopes to determine the first event of the evening. In the midst of each activity, have your date open another envelope to reveal the location of the next event. Continue the process until you and your date—or the envelopes—are exhausted.

If you have more time and plenty of film, you can categorize your dating activities: dinners, desserts, entertainment, sports, sites, and gifts. Have several photographs in each category portraying the different options. The selection process is more exciting in this version, because your date may choose only one envelope from each category. While the two of you are sit-

What to Do If You Are Stood Up

It happens. Your date calls and cancels the one thing you have been looking forward to all week. Or worse yet, your date doesn't call, leaving you confused, angry, and alone. If you should happen to be stood up, console yourself by considering one of the following options:

- Think about how much money you are saving.
- Realize that you now have time to get to that item that has been on your "to do" list for ages.
- Write the person a note saying, "Dear _____, I went out by my-

ting in a fast-food restaurant you photographed, let your date open the other "Dinners" envelopes to find out where you *could* have been dining.

> self last night and met the person of my dreams. Thanks for making the opportunity possible."
> - Sharpen your darts and look for a photo.
> - Send your date a book on etiquette.
> - Call up the person's best friend and ask for a date.
> - Booby trap your date's front door so that a bucket of cold water will provide a welcome upon arrival. Make the bucket big enough for two, in case you were stood up for someone else.
> - Send your date this form letter:
>
>> Dear _____:
>> I am writing you this note to tell you
>> ☐ thanks.
>> ☐ that you are a jerk.
>> ☐ that you owe me one hundred dollars for standing me up.
>> I also wanted to let you know that I
>> ☐ cried all night.
>> ☐ had a great time with someone else.
>> The next time you need to stand me up,
>> ☐ give me two days' notice.
>> ☐ drop dead.
>> ☐ I will have another great time with someone else.
>> Well, that is about all I have to say at this point.
>>
>>> ☐ Love and kisses,
>>> ☐ Sincerely,
>>> ☐ Signed,

Intimate Ice Cream

Make arrangements with the manager of an ice-cream parlor to rent the shop to you and your date for thirty minutes after closing. Since the workers will be there cleaning up anyway, it is simple for the manager to make the necessary arrangements. Since the place is yours for half an hour, try to work some of these activities into the agenda:

- Have an ice-cream-eating contest.
- Give your blindfolded date a taste test with spoonfuls of ice cream to see how many flavors he or she can identify.
- Feed each other.
- Ask each other trivia questions: the loser in each

round must eat another scoop. (The last one to get sick wins the game.)
- Mix ice cream to invent new flavors.
- Build a snowman.
- Eat with your fingers.
- See how much ice cream you can get in your mouth, then say, "Abominable Snowman."
- Sink your teeth into large bites of ice cream and see who can last the longest.
- Ask if you can scrape clean the empty cartons.

3.

Outrageously Expensive Dates

This chapter is written for two groups of people. The first group is very small indeed and consists of those who have enough money to actually try these ideas. The majority of us, however, fit into the second group: Either we save for years to try out just one of these dates on a special person with whom we intend to spend the rest of our lives, or we merely imagine experiencing one of them without actually spending anything.

The last date in this chapter is written in great detail, to give you an example of how any date—no matter what the cost—can be expanded to include many unforgettable extras that add a personal touch to the adventure.

Skyscraper Rentals

Restaurants with spectacular views of the city can be found at the tops of tall hotels and office buildings in many large cities. To enjoy the sights in an intimate way, arrange to have your own private dinner on the roof of a tall building. If you or someone you know leases space in or owns a suitable building, these arrangements will be relatively simple. If you have no connections, you will have to deal with the building owner or leasing agent.

Hire a full-service caterer to provide the meal (and the furniture to eat on), and book a small band or ensemble to provide the background and dancing music. If the evenings tend to get breezy, you may wish to hold the party indoors in one of the top floor offices; connections are virtually a must for this type of arrangement.

To put a spectacular close to the evening, try this. Explain to your date that you had lost track of time and that the building's elevators have automatically shut down to discourage burglaries. Without a special override key to activate the lifts, the two of you will have to walk down the fire stairs. As you take a few minutes to watch the city below before beginning your long walk down, notice a helicopter flying by (which you have prearranged). Wave frantically at it as if you are in trouble, making a joke that the two of you may not have to walk down after all. Of course, the helicopter will circle and land; the two of you will climb aboard and instantly be whisked away from your dinner spot. After an aerial tour of the city, have the pilot set you down somewhere closer to street level. Be certain to tell the musicians and caterers that the elevator story was false: it is difficult to negotiate seven thousand steps while carrying a cello or a dining table.

Off the Rack

A delightful way to dress up for a night on the town with your date is to select a wardrobe for each other that will complement you as a couple. On the day of your date, go shopping together. Tell your friend that you want the evening to be special and that each of you is to select a complete outfit. For her, this means a dress, shoes, purse, and other accessories. For him, this means slacks, shirt, coat, tie, belt, socks, and shoes.

When suitable outfits have been chosen, purchase and wear them out of the store (be sure to remove the tags). Go directly to your first engagement of the evening. Without exception, the two of you will be wearing the latest outfits of anyone there.

Table for Two

Plan to celebrate a special anniversary by having a very exclusive dinner. A few hours before you wish to eat, take your date to a nice department store. Explain that you would like to buy some new dishes and things, but only want to try two place settings to see if you like them before purchasing a complete set. Go from department to department selecting and purchasing the following items:

- Two place settings of china (Aynsley is nice.)
- Two place settings of crystal stemware (Baccarat is a good name.)
- Two place settings of silver flatware (Try Gorham or Kirk-Stieff.)
- A set of fine table linens including a tablecloth and napkins

- A set of silver or crystal candleholders and candles
- A pair of silver napkin rings

Since it would be foolish to leave your newly purchased treasures in the car while you go to a restaurant to eat, drive home to put everything away. You and your date will be greeted at your door by the chef you have hired who is eager to set the table with your purchases. You may then relax and enjoy an intimate meal together at a table spread for the occasion.

How to Make an Impressive Entrance

Communication experts say that the image you convey during the first thirty seconds of meeting someone becomes the substance of the person's overall impression of you. When you really want that initial impression to be spectacular, try one of these:

- Gallop up to her door on a black stallion.
- Parachute into his backyard.
- Free-fall into her hot tub.
- Arrive on motorized roller skates.
- Shoot yourself onto his porch from a cannon.
- Slide down the chute of a cement truck.
- Get spit-out of the belly of a whale. (This has been done before.)
- Ride up to his door on the back of a Bengal tiger.
- Rappel onto her apartment balcony from the roof.
- Tunnel up through his kitchen floor.

To celebrate the anniversary each year, pull out this special set of china, silver, crystal, and linen, which is used only on this date. Look at this eccentric purchase as an investment in a long-lasting tradition.

Intimate Yachting

In many marinas, a variety of handsome sailing and motor vessels may be chartered complete with captain and crew. Depending on your plans and pocketbook, a yacht from twenty to two hundred feet in length will

- Swing through her window on the wrecking ball of a crane.
- Roll up to his house balanced on a medicine ball.
- Provoke a professional wrestler to body-slam you onto her lawn.
- Have five trumpeters announce your arrival with horns.
- Crawl down the chimney in a red velvet suit.

meet your needs. A carefully planned trip can include an afternoon of sailing, deck lounging, or fishing; a sunset-illuminated dinner, and an evening view of the harbor lights.

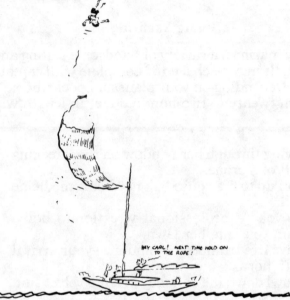

HEY CARL! NEXT TIME HOLD ON TO THE ROPE!

If weather and water conditions permit, try some of these activities:

- *Swimming, Snorkeling, Scuba Diving:* Have your captain anchor in a clear, safe place away from boat traffic.
- *Spinnaker Flying:* If you are aboard a sailing vessel, try this special thrill while anchored. A flotation life preserver is rigged to the bottom of this balloon-like sail, whose top corner is attached to the mast. To ride the sail, the flyer sits on the life preserver while it floats on the water. When the sail fills with a gust of wind, the seat and its occupant are pulled high into the air. If the wind drops, so does the flyer.

- *Board Sailing:* Rent a couple of sailboards and stow them on deck before shoving off. If neither of you has tried this combination surfing and sailing sport, bring along an instructor.
- *Water-skiing:* See if the charter company has a ski boat that can be towed behind the larger vessel. If the water is too rough to ski, tie an inner tube to the end of the ski rope, and ride the bouncing tube as it is pulled behind the boat.

Single-Day Skiing

If a busy schedule prevents you from spending much time skiing this winter, make plans for a one-day ski adventure. Charter a small jet to fly you and your

date to the mountains. Upon arrival, you will be greeted by your personal guide, who will treat you to a day of helicopter skiing. In many resort areas, heli-skiing trips can be reserved for a private party. Once aboard the helicopter, the pilot will fly the two of you over beautiful and remote terrain to the top of your all-day ski run. Your day actually begins here, as you charge through fresh powder on deserted slopes, halt-ing occasionally to catch, not a chairlift, but your breath. The guide will treat you to the best of the mountain, and if arranged, take photographs of your descent.

At the bottom, you will be escorted back to civiliza-tion, where you may wish to have an early dinner fol-lowed by a stroll through town. Catch a ride out to the airport at a prearranged time to board your private flight home.

Helicopter Dating

If you can afford to rent one, a helicopter can be an extremely exciting and memorable way to travel on a date. When making reservations, ask if the charter company knows of any romantic spots where the heli-copter can land, such as a remote beach, meadow, or hilltop. If the company knows of a spot where the view of the sunset is especially beautiful, arrange your flight to begin just before the sun goes down. Here are some other ideas for helicopter dates:

- *Car Trouble:* Take your date for a drive in the coun-try. On an isolated stretch of road pretend that you are having car trouble. Pull over, check under the hood, and mutter something about a broken hose and a tow truck. As the two of you are walking to a phone, a helicopter will pass overhead. Stick your thumb out as if you are a hitchiker. When the aircraft circles back to land, shout with amazement. Run up to the helicopter, and ask the pilot for a lift to a phone. When the two of you are inside and buckled up, the pilot will suggest that if you are not in too great a hurry to get to a phone, he or she would be happy to give you an aerial tour. Following an exciting thirty-minute flight, you will be dropped off at your car. When your date reminds you that you still have not phoned for help, matter-of-factly explain that the car is not broken and that the whole adventure was a setup.

- *Double Trouble:* To make things even more unbelievable, have a friend and his or her date "break down" on another nearby road. A few minutes after you and your companion have been picked up by the considerate pilot, look down at a car parked by the side of a road, and say that the car looks like your friend's. When the pilot goes down for a closer look, recognize your friend and ask the pilot to land. While your and your friend's dates look bewildered, you and your friend will feign astonishment for as long as the whole trick goes undiscovered (which will not be long at this point). The four of you then complete the aerial tour before each couple is eventually dropped off at their car.

Both of these dates require extensive communication with the pilot beforehand to ensure that all will go as planned. The next idea is less complex and more romantic.

- *Fly and Dine:* Make reservations for dinner at the restaurant of a hotel with a helipad. Have the helicopter fly you and your date to and from dinner. You may wish to hop from one activity to the next via the aircraft so that you can have before-dinner refreshments at one establishment and dinner at another, finishing with dessert at a third. To cut down on the hourly charge, fly one way only. Take in a sunset flight before dinner, and dismiss the pilot upon arrival at the restaurant. After the meal, return by less expensive ground transportation such as a taxi or limousine.

- *Air Tours:* In many picturesque areas of the country, helicopter companies have air tours that last anywhere from three minutes to an hour. Since most charters have a one-hour minimum charge, this type of flight may be the most economical way to enjoy the thrill of helicopter dating.

Private Showing

Rather than fight the crowds to see a major motion picture when it is first released, arrange a time for your own showing. Contact the theater manager to de-

termine a time that is suitable. The best times are on weekday afternoons before the theater opens and late in the evening after the last showing. Expect to pay for the cost of staffing the theater, along with any of the fees associated with the showing of the film itself.

Since such showings are rare, you will probably want to make the most of it. Arrive at the show in a limousine, have a photographer greet you at the curb for photos, and arrange to partake in exclusive snacks like gourmet popcorn, french chocolates, and cherry colas served in crystal glasses. The evening will be a complete success if you take care of one extremely important detail—make sure that your date wants to see that particular movie!

Breakfast Plus

Treat your date to a special day that will be long remembered. Hire a limousine to take you to your date's house to pick her up for an early-morning breakfast. Be sure to have the driver use your camera to take some photographs of the two of you getting into the car. The limousine is her first clue that this will be an extraordinary breakfast; her second clue comes when you arrive at the airport.

Explain that you know of an exceptional place for breakfast in your destination city and felt like eating there this morning. Sit in the boarding area, near a bank of pay phones. When one of the pay phones begins to ring, go and answer it. With a bewildered look, tell your date that the caller wants to speak to her. When she picks up the phone, your date will be greeted by a family member or roommate who wishes her a pleasant trip and assures her that if she is gone longer than breakfast, she will not cause any worry. After hanging up, your date will have guessed that you actually came to the airport a few days earlier to jot down phone numbers and had instructed her family member or friend to dial one of the phone numbers at the correct time.

During your flight, you may wish to serve a small snack to tide the two of you over until breakfast; bring along freshly squeezed orange juice and some croissants. Have a flight attendant photograph the two of you with your camera to record the flight. Upon arrival, you are greeted by a person holding a small, white sign with your name on it. He is your chauffeur, who leads you out to his waiting limousine. Stepping inside the car, your date finds a rose and an envelope containing a card which you have written. (You have sent the card to the limousine company instructing them to place the envelope and a rose on the seat.)

Your first destination of the morning is the breakfast place you have flown such a distance to dine at. During breakfast, you suggest that since you have come this far you may as well make a day of it. Your chauffeur takes you to various sights throughout the city on a VIP tour. Take plenty of photographs, using up the roll of film. One of the stops is an area where you can do some window shopping. Take careful note of any items that your date seems to show a special interest in; you will arrange later on to see that she receives one of them as a gift.

A little later, stop for lunch at a previously selected restaurant near a park. You have arranged to have a friend who lives in the city—and whom your date has never met—meet you at the beginning of your lunch. When you notice your accomplice enter, excuse yourself to the restroom. After saying hello, hand him the roll of film from the morning, a business card, two cards in envelopes, a description of the gift that you saw while window shopping, and some money. Tell him exactly where your limousine is parked and when and where you will rendezvous again; then return to your date.

After lunch, walk down the street for ice-cream cones, and then take a leisurely stroll through the park. After a while, take a rest on a bench. While the two of you are sitting there, your accomplice appears out of nowhere dressed in a formal waiter's uniform, balancing in his hand a silver tray containing a tall bottle of chilled refreshment and two crystal glasses. You pretend not to recognize your accomplice, who proceeds to serve you and your date with professional grace. Before departing, he places the tray between you on the bench. Upon the tray, your date notices another rose and an envelope. Opening the envelope, she discovers a card signed by you and a photograph of the two of you at her house standing by the first limousine.

While you empty your glass and she ponders the complexity of this last surprise, your accomplice returns, this time carrying a wrapped gift. He trades the gift for the tray and disappears. Your date opens the package to find the very item she had shown interest in that morning. Before your date has time to figure out how this encounter in the park was arranged, return to your limousine to continue the adventure.

(Here is how you arranged the park encounter: When your friend left the restaurant, he went around the corner to where you had instructed the chauffeur to park. To identify himself, he showed your business card to the driver—who was instructed by your note to follow the directions of your friend. He then directed the driver to a nearby one-hour photo processing lab. After leaving your film there, he was driven to the store to purchase the gift. After purchasing the gift [which the store wrapped] with the money you gave him, your friend returned to the lab to pick up the prints. Enroute to the park, he took one of the prints and placed it in an envelope, putting the rest of the prints and negatives beneath the seat for you to recover later. He was dropped off at his car near the park, where he put on his tie and coat. He pulled the rose and bottle from an ice chest, placed everything on the tray, and left his car with the gift hidden inside. After serving you the tray, he returned to his car to get the gift. Following the presentation of the gift, he took the tray back to his car. A bit complex, but first class surprises often are.)

After a few more hours of sights, you and your companion go to dinner at a very nice restaurant where you have made reservations. Upon your table, your date discovers another rose and envelope. The envelope contains a note and a photograph of the two of you being served in the park. She will be pleased to know that the encounter was recorded on film and yet hopelessly perplexed at how you have managed to do so.

(The last surprise was made possible in this way: Your accomplice had an assistant with him who was equipped with a camera with a telephoto lens. As you and your date were sitting on the park bench, this assistant photographed the entire sequence, capturing each look of amazement and every disbelieving smile. Following the park scene, your accomplice had this roll of film developed at the lab. He took the best shot, placed it in the second envelope you had given him during lunch, and then delivered the envelope and rose to the restaurant where you would soon arrive for dinner. Waiting outside the restaurant, he saw the two of you go inside and walked up to the limousine to place the remainder of the prints beneath the seat along with the first prints.)

Your chauffeur drives you to the airport immediately following dinner. You discreetly retrieve your photographs from beneath the seat and depart. The arrival back at your own airport is made special by another driver who takes you to a limousine. Your date discovers another rose and envelope when she steps inside the car. (You had made these arrangements before arriving at your date's house earlier that day.)

After saying good night at her door, you are driven home. Meanwhile, your date has gone to her bedroom to find one dozen roses and another envelope. The note inside thanks her for having "breakfast" with you and wishes her pleasant dreams. (You had made arrangements with a roommate or family member to set these out.)

When she steps into her car to drive to school or work the next morning, she reads a note taped to her steering wheel telling her to play the cassette in her car stereo. The tape contains a recording of you, wishing her a good morning and telling her to look in the car trunk. When she does, she discovers a rose and a box. The box contains a photo album chronicling the previous day's adventures. It includes plane tickets, limousine service brochures, postcards of the city, dried rose petals, matchbooks from restaurants, and, of course, photographs from the rolls already developed. The album contains a few blank pages which will be filled with the prints not yet developed. On one note is an invitation to breakfast so that the two of you can complete the album. (After being dropped off at home, you put the photographs and souvenirs in a photo album you had purchased. You had also dried a rose earlier in the week to include in the album. You drove to your date's car very early the next morning to set everything up. The cassette was recorded earlier in the week. To get into the car, you got a spare key from a roommate or had one made the day you offered to wash and wax her car.)

In the mail the next week she will receive a postcard from you sent from the destination city. (Your accomplice had given you the card to sign and address when you met him in the restaurant.)

If you are able to plan this date carefully beforehand, the joy of seeing the production come together will be nearly as great as the unforgettable times you will have enjoyed with your companion. When all is finished, do not forget to generously thank your friend and accomplice who made the magic possible. Offer to return the favor when he takes his date to your town for breakfast.

Checklist

One month beforehand:

☐ 1. Make breakfast date with your special friend.
☐ 2. Reserve date with accomplice in destination city.
☐ 3. Inform your date's roommate or family member of plans so that they will help keep the day open in your date's calendar.
☐ 4. Book flights.
☐ 5. Book limousines.
☐ 6. Write detailed agenda.
☐ 7. Get spare key to your date's car.

One week beforehand:

☐ 1. Write all six cards; mail card #1 to limousine company in destination city with instructions.
☐ 2. Make dinner reservations at restaurant.
☐ 3. Mail agenda to accomplice.
☐ 4. Purchase photo album, film, and blank cassette tape.
☐ 5. Record message on cassette.
☐ 6. Give card #5 to your date's roommate, along with money for one dozen roses.
☐ 7. Make note to be taped to steering wheel.

The day beforehand:

☐ 1. Purchase rose to be put in car with photo album.

☐ 2. Prepare money.
☐ 3. Prepare in-flight snack if needed.
☐ 4. Prepare note for first chauffeur; attach card #4 to be placed with rose after return flight.
☐ 5. Prepare note for second chauffeur, explaining the arrangements with your accomplice.
☐ 6. Confirm limousine reservations.
☐ 7. Pack cards, notes, agenda, and tickets.
☐ 8. Confirm time with your date.

That day:

☐ 1. Call to confirm flight.
☐ 2. Give first chauffeur card #4 and note explaining the card and rose placement (before arriving at your date's house).
☐ 3. Slip second chauffeur note explaining arrangements with accomplice.
☐ 4. Collect matchbooks and other souvenirs throughout the day.
☐ 5. Shoot a complete roll of film by lunchtime.
☐ 6. Take note of a gift that pleases your date.
☐ 7. Rendezvous with accomplice in restaurant. Give him cards #2 and #3, business card, location and description of gift, first roll of film, and money for gift and film developing. Sign and address postcard and give back to him.
☐ 8. Retrieve prints from beneath seat before departing for flight home.
☐ 9. Put together scrapbook when you get home.

The next morning:

☐ 1. Very early, take spare key, album, rose, note #6, steering-wheel note, and cassette tape to her car and set up final surprise.

☐ 2. Call accomplice, thank profusely; offer to return favor.

☐ 3. Take undeveloped rolls to be developed.

4.

49 Creative Ways to Say
I Love You

1. Write it on a steamy mirror—timing is important.
2. Fill his office, room, or car with balloons saying, "I love you."
3. Spell it on her desk with jelly beans or green M&Ms.
4. Put it on a billboard.

5. Spell it with birdseed on his lawn.
6. Say it in a foreign language.
7. Paint it on a banner and hang it on the garage door.
8. Leave "I love you" notes to be discovered days later (e.g., lawn mower, sewing machine, casserole in the freezer).
9. Carve it in balsa wood and set it afloat in the toilet.
10. Hang an "I love you" note in front of a doorway.
11. Paint it in the bathtub with food coloring (depend-

ing on the type of bathtub, this could be a permanent message).

12. Have a disc jockey dedicate a song saying "I love you" (make sure he's listening).
13. Hire an airplane to pull a banner that says "I love you." Or if you just happen to see one, claim it as yours.
14. Bake it in a fortune cookie.
15. Use a talking bird to say it.
16. Write it on your eyelids and shut your eyes.
17. Plant a garden that spells "I love you" (use only in long-term relationships).
18. Write a book and say it in the dedication.
19. Leave it on a phone recorder.
20. Bury an "I love you" treasure and provide her with a map.
21. Rearrange his house to make it appear as if someone broke in. Leave an "I love you" note on the phone, which he will discover when he goes to call the police. Caution: make sure he has a great sense of humor.
22. Communicate it with sign language.
23. Pop your head into her class, office, etc. to catch her off guard and quickly say, "I love you."
24. Spell it with rocks in the bottom of a pool.
25. Sprinkle the words "I love you" with baby powder on her carpet.
26. Write it on his calendar on various days.
27. Place bamboo shoots under your fingernails and run into the room screaming, "Okay, okay, I love you!"
28. Trim the initials "I L Y" into her shrubbery (make sure you have the correct address).
29. Carve it in clay and place it in his medicine cabinet.
30. Shave "I love you" onto the fur of her pet Alsatian (make sure the dog shares your sense of humor).
31. Inscribe it on the inside of his mirrored sunglasses.

Use a paint brush, engraving marker, soldering iron, glass cutter, oxyacetlyene torch, or masking tape.

32. Carve it into the side of his barn with a chain saw.
33. Cut and paste printed words together into an anonymous "I love you" note.
34. Brand it into his polo pony (this could be an expensive way to show your love).

35. Weave "I love you" with ribbon into the strings of her racquetball or tennis racquet.
36. During a movie theater intermission have the projectionist flash a previously prepared slide saying,

---

One of the World's Worst Dates #1

August 3, 1985: Boulder, Colorado

Mike Driggs picked up Pam Sears for what he thought would be an enjoyable dinner date. After getting themselves completely lost looking for an out-of-town restaurant, Mike's car ran out of gas (not on purpose). Walking almost two miles to a service station, the couple borrowed a gas can and hitched a ride back down the road with the tow truck driver. Upon returning to the spot where they had left the car, they discovered that it had been stolen. Back at the service station, they waited forty-five minutes for the police to arrive and another two hours for the completion of the police report. A twenty-dollar cab ride got the couple to an airport car rental agency. Seemingly undaunted, Mike insisted on going to dinner. When they came out of the restaurant, Mike was informed that the parking valet had backed the rented car into a guardrail. To make matters worse, on the way to Pam's house they got ticketed for not having brake lights. After receiving the invitation to come into Pam's house, Mike opened the front door only to be greeted by a bite on the arm from Pam's German shepherd. The bite required eight stitches, which he received in the emergency room at one o'clock in the morning.

THE OUTCOME: Mike received a job with the car rental agency, and Pam wound up dating the intern in the emergency room.

"I love you Cathy" (use only if her name is Cathy).

37. Use your saliva to spell it on her clean window.
38. Buy an advertisement and declare it in the local newspaper.
39. Throw dirt clods (or snowballs) against her garage door until it spells "I love you."
40. Send it in a letter or telegram.
41. Mail it electronically to her company computer.
42. Lay out several postcards next to each other and write one big "I love you," using one letter per card. Mail each postcard a week apart. If you don't believe in long-term relationships, mail one per day, and if that's too long—use bulk mail.

Holiday "I Love You's"

43. *New Year's:* Scream it in her ear at 12:01 A.M.
44. *Valentine's Day:* Buy him this book.
45. *Easter:* Melt chocolate eggs to spell it on her kitchen floor.

46. *Fourth of July:* Set "I L Y" ablaze with sparklers on his porch. For added meaning, underline sparklers with black snakes, outline with fire crackers, emphasize with Roman candles—you get the point.
47. *Halloween:* Write it with fake blood on her mirror.
48. *Thanksgiving:* Stuff the turkey with a note saying "I love you" and listing reasons why you are thankful for him.
49. *Christmas:* Make an "I love you" ornament.

5.

Group Dates

One way to add variety to your dating life and to spend quality time with other friends is to date with other couples. Group dating is ideal on a number of occasions: when you may not yet feel comfortable alone with your date, when pooling resources allows you to do more for your money, or when activities call for more than two people. Your friends will be delighted to accompany you on any dating adventure you create from the ideas listed in this chapter.

THE MAN SAID, JUST POKE AROUND THE GARAGE AND TAKE WHAT YOU'D LIKE....

Can You Top This?

Each couple in the group is given a toothpick and instructed to go out into the neighborhood and exchange the item for something better. Going from door to door, they ask the residents, "Can you top this?" At the first house they will trade the toothpick for anything better that the occupant is willing to give away. The couple then takes this item to another house and tries to exchange it for something even better. The exchanging goes on until the time is up. All the couples then return to their starting point to see which couple struck it rich. Your pogo stick, broken television, bed post, swing set, or other item of junk can be saved, bronzed, sold, or given to a charitable cause.

The Wedding Party

Wives love to participate in this one, since it gives them the opportunity to wear their wedding dress at least one more time. Gather your married friends together and have a wedding party. The wives will wear their dresses, and the men will rent tuxedoes (rent them as a group for a better price). Have a wedding cake, wedding music, and wedding decorations. Each couple should bring their wedding album along with any funny stories about their special day or honeymoon. Have each couple dig through their closets to find their most ridiculous wedding gift (make sure that the giver will not be in attendance), and exchange these at the party.

Wedding-day memories are special, and a wedding party gives each couple the opportunity to relive and share some of those memories.

Home Movies

Rather than go out to the movies, have each couple bring a movie over to the house. Some can bring home movies; others can check out comedy shorts or cartoons from the library. Show them simultaneously on different walls within the house. In addition to projectors, be sure to provide a movie atmosphere with popcorn, lemonade, and bonbons. (If you like, spill sodas before the guests arrive to give your floors that authentic sticky feel.)

Cow Tipping

This rural prank can make a very adventurous group date. Few people happen to know that most cows love to be pushed over while standing.* The object of this date is to break up into couples and see how

many cows each pair can topple. A few cautions: (1) Make sure the cow is actually one of those we interviewed; (2) make sure the animal you intend to push over is a cow, not a bull; (3) be careful the cow is not filled with explosives; and (4) make sure that the cow's owner is not standing nearby with a shotgun.

Group Meals

Instead of having one couple cook for all the others, have each couple cook different portions of one meal. Instead of a progressive dinner have a *regressive* meal—where everyone meets at the first house for dessert, drives to the next house for the main dish, goes to

---

*At least most of the cows we talked to.

the next for salad, and visits the last for appetizers. For another kind of variety, have each couple prepare a different ethnic dish and take a world tour. If you are a daring bunch, you might want to try one of these innovative meals:

- *Aggressive Dinner:* Just one place setting is set and the group fights over who gets to eat.

- *Repressive Dinner:* All are served food they were forced to eat as children but have long since tried to forget.
- *Resistive Dinner:* Everyone takes one bite and then does not want to eat any more.
- *Repetitive Dinner:* Bake a meat loaf and serve it at each portion of the meal: meat loaf appetizer, meat loaf salad, meat loaf meat loaf, meat loaf dessert.
- *Reparative Dinner:* After taking a bite, offer suggestions how the dish could be prepared better. (Do not be surprised if you are not asked back.)

Putting Heads Together

Sometimes an activity can cost more than each couple can afford to spend. Depending on your finances, a play, ski trip, cruise, or vacation in Europe may be just out of reach. To obtain the extra cash needed to treat yourselves to something special, hold a fund-raiser. If your group wants to go on a weekend cruise, throw a precruise party to discuss the fund-raising effort. Set a goal of how much money needs to be raised, and then list all the ways the group can reach the goal.

Pool everyone's unwanted possessions together and have a precruise garage sale. Host a precruise car wash, and sell tickets to it at each person's office or school. Or set up a free car wash, and put up signs throughout the neighborhood telling people about it. Make sure your entire group is there with plenty of water, soap, and rags, because there will be quite a line of bargain hunters with dirty cars. Adjacent to where the cars are being washed set up a box with a hole in the top. A sign above it explains why you are washing cars and invites people to support the cause with a dona-

WE WANT TO THROW A PARTY AND NEED SOME EXTRA MONEY.

tion. Hint: the cleaner the cars turn out, the sooner your group will be on a cruise.

Depending on the talents of your group's members, you can hold precruise bake, crafts, or plant and flower sales or host a tennis, golf, or racquetball tournament. Such activities are also great for getting the group excited about the trip and for giving members an ideal opportunity to get to know each other better. It may turn out that the pretrip activities are more fun than the trip itself.

Group Efforts

If, in putting your heads together, you and your friends stumble upon an effective fund-raising scheme, put your energies together again and raise money for a worthy cause such as these:

• Hungry people
• Disabled children
• Disease research
• Rehabilitation centers

There are countless causes that deserve your support, and the results of your teamwork will pay dividends that cannot be measured.

Parading Friends

Who says there has to be a special event or a holiday to have a parade? Get some friends together, and plan your own. Map out a parade route, and decide on costumes to wear and instruments to play (you do not have to be musicians; use anything that makes noise). Here are some parade ideas:

• *Radio March:* Ask a local music station to play parade music during a specific time of the day. Each parade member brings along a portable radio and marches to the music being played. Invite passing

drivers and curbside spectators to tune in and join the band.

- *Kazoo Parade:* Have everyone purchase this funny-sounding instrument, and let your parade hum. If your group can afford some extra kazoos, bring them along to pass out to onlookers.
- *Float Competition:* Different couples can decorate wagons, shopping carts, and bicycles and enter them into the parade under various categories. Toy music instruments can be played by "bands" to separate the floats.

The smiles, cheers, and laughter of spectators will convince you it's true: People love a parade.

Day Camp

Invite several couples to a picnic in the park. Rent a school bus with driver and pick up each person at home. Give out demerits to anyone who eats on the bus. When you arrive at the park, pass out playground equipment like frisbees, jump ropes, and kickballs. When it is time to go, give awards to those who pick up the most trash, and have the bus driver signal that it is time to leave by honking the horn three times. Make a last minute sweep of the picnic site for sweaters and purses; put these in the lost and found box. When the bus is loaded, call roll from a clipboard. Drop off all the passengers at their doorsteps, and pin notes on their shirts telling their parents how well behaved they were.

Mud Slinging

Wear old clothes and take a trip to a nearby mud hole. Let your imagination go wild with all the things you can do:

- Start off by covering each other with mud from head to toe to get everyone comfortable.
- If the mud is thick enough, make mud sculptures.
- Play football or any variation of it.
- Run up to the mud hole and then slide, seeing how far you go before bogging down.
- If you are close to a street where other people can see what you are doing, set up an old card table and chairs, make mud pies, and pretend to eat them as you sit there covered in muck.

PREPARING & TESTING WORLD-CLASS MUD PUDDLE

- Have "drag races": each person drags a partner through the mud track.
- Pair off and do some tag-team mud wrestling. Award points based on drama rather than ability.

Some very funny things can result from this event. Be sure not to surprise your friends with this one (unless they are crazy by nature); most people need to get psyched up for this one. But when they do—there is mud everywhere.

Theme Night

With just a few couples and a creative theme this party date can be the hit of the year. Try one of these themes or invent your own:

Banana Night	Disney Night
Hillbilly Night	Celebrity Night
Sports Night	Elite Night
Baby Night	Color/Pattern Night
1800s Night	

Make sure that everything you do is related in some way to your chosen theme. If you plan to host a Banana Night, dry banana peels and write the invitations on them. Each couple must wear yellow, prepare a dish made with bananas, and bring a bunch of bananas. Serve fried banana chips, banana bread, banana malts, and a banana casserole (if you can figure out how). Activities for the evening can include the following:

- *Banana-Eating Contest:* See who can eat the fastest, the most, and the largest amount in one bite.
- *Couples' Competition:* Have couples put their

arms behind their backs and eat their way to the middle of a banana.

- *Bob for Bananas:* Why wait until Halloween for this party favorite? Apples are too easy anyway.
- *Stories:* Instead of ghost stories, tell banana stories. Use an encyclopedia for interesting facts and trivia.
- *Banana Splits:* Of course the party would not be complete without a large banana split.
- *Banana T.P.:* Instead of wasting toilet paper, hang your leftover banana peels on your friends' trees.

Your theme night will be limited only by your ability to be creative. To help you imagine what the evening could include, make a list of everything that you associate with the chosen theme. Write down movies, songs, books, games, foods, activities, clothing, sounds—anything that pops into your head. Go through the list again and ask yourself, "How can I incorporate this idea into the evening?" Some of the items on the list will not work or can be dropped because of a better idea, but the completed list will provide you with material for a very creative party.

Dye Wars
Gather your group and head to a park or wooded area. Each person needs to wear a white T-shirt and

have a squirt gun. Divide into red and blue teams. The red team fills their guns with red food coloring and water, and the blue team puts blue food coloring and water in their weapons. The object of the game is to shoot the other team's players before they shoot you. Once a player is shot, he or she is out. The team with the last person standing wins. After the shooting stops have a picnic. Don't worry about spilling food on your shirts.

Car Rally

There are many different types of car rallies throughout the world, but they all share a common denominator—fun.

For a car rally, divide your group into teams, and assign each team a car. Each team drives around, following a list of instructions, clues, or questions that will give them a chance of winning.

One rally idea is to give each team (or car) a sheet of clues that will take them around the surrounding area. For example, the sheet might instruct the team to "turn left out of the parking lot, go until you get to 'president,' then turn left on 'famous explorer' until you reach '$8 \times 4 \div 2 + 5 + 0$,' then turn right into the 'lighted arches' for your next clue" (Lincoln Street, Columbus, 21st, and McDonald's would be the answers). To make things more interesting, have the list include questions that must be answered in order to win: "How many trees are on the left-hand side of Walnut Street?"; "How many banks do you pass?"; or "What movie is playing at the local cinema?" Assign points to each task based on the degree of difficulty.

In another rally, each car is given an instant camera and a list of things to photograph. Reward each photograph with points depending on the degree of difficulty:

- The team on a diving board (100 points); high dive (200 points)
- The team in front of a bank clock at 8:03 (300 points)
- The team trying on shoes in a department store (400 points)
- The team in a fire engine (500 points)
- The team milking a cow (600 points); if you live in the country (100 points); if you live in India (10,000 points)
- The team cooking french fries at a fast-food restaurant (500 points)
- The team toilet-papering a police car (1,000 points)
- The team in the cockpit of an airplane (2,000 points)
- The team jumping off a ten-story building (disqualification)

These photographs will be a constant reminder of the laughs that were shared and the crazy poses attempted.

If you don't have time to plan one of these rallies, try

a "spontaneous rally." Just before everyone gets in the cars, make some things up such as "The first one back with a small, medium, and large cup from Wendy's, twenty yellow pencils, a tennis racquet, and a half gallon of ice cream wins." When the teams return, eat the

---

One of the World's Worst Dates #2

September 12, 1981: Los Angeles, California

Jeff Genoway and Doug Webster took their dates to a college football game. At halftime all four quickly made their way to the snack bar and then to the restrooms. When the guys finished, they waited outside the women's restroom for their dates. After fifteen minutes the guys, anxious to see the second half kickoff, began looking into the women's restroom doorway to tell one of the girls (who might be waiting around) that they were going back to their seats. Since they did not see the girls, they began to shout the girls' names. The university police spotted the guys in the doorway to the restroom and immediately escorted them out of the stadium. When the girls came out and could not find their dates, they concluded that they had been ditched. They left the game in anger and had to call a friend to get a ride home. When the guys managed to call their dates later that night, they tried to explain what had happened. At first skeptical, the girls were finally convinced that the ridiculous story was true.

THE OUTCOME: The girls have never again attended a football game, and the guys . . . well, never mind.

---

ice cream and watch the classic movie *The Gumball Rally* on a video.

If for some reason your group cannot use cars, try using buses, subways, or bicycles.

When planning a car rally, be sure to stress safe driving. If the teams are big, have one member ride with another team and take off points every time the speed limit is exceeded. Seal each person's driver's license in an envelope and hand it back. At the end of the rally, check the envelopes to see that none had to be opened because the driver was pulled over.

6.

Asking Someone Out

Many people do not date because of the fear associated with the asking. We have attempted to alleviate some of that anxiety by providing you with proven alternatives to the cliché line, "Are you busy Friday night?" For those of you who have no fear, try some of the more outlandish ideas listed. REMEMBER: creative dates start with the asking.

The Presentation

This method works well if you have access to a private office or conference room. Ask your date-to-be to

step into the room to hear a presentation. In a very business-like manner, you present a dating proposal. Start your presentation by inviting the person to pay close attention to your short but important message. Use a flipchart, easel, and pointer to display your visual aids, and have a well-prepared set of charts, graphs, and illustrations to keep things interesting. These might include the following:

- *Options Chart:* List several possible activities available should the date be accepted. The chart can include "pluses" and "minuses" to each idea.
- *Cost Analysis:* List the various activities and graph them according to cost. The number of pennies taped in a line can correspond to the relative expense of each date.
- *Enjoyment Curve:* Graphically plot the increase in enjoyment the person will receive over time as a result of the date. Other curves plotted on the same graph can represent a date with a total creep and no date at all.
- *Time Line:* Illustrate the days you are available for a date. At this point, you will need to "close" the sale by asking your date-to-be to select a date and an activity. When a date has been agreed to and an activity has been decided upon, shake hands to conclude the deal.

If your presentation fails to land you a date, then *(a)* go home and polish up your sales pitch, *(b)* try a new person, or *(c)* wait around until someone calls you.

Making News

If you have access to a video cassette recorder and camera, try filming a personal request.

While you and your prospective date are watching some previously recorded program being played on the VCR, the show will be interrupted by a special news bulletin (which you have taped over a portion of the show). Suddenly you appear on the screen, asking for a date. With some imagination, you can create a very clever and effective news brief. Of course, if your prospective date walks out in the middle of the show, you have your answer.

Reading the Fine Print

Have a friend disguised as a delivery person take a fake package to your prospective date's home. The delivery person will see to it that your prospect signs an "acknowledgement of receipt" document which you have had printed beforehand (see document below). Your friend will behave as if in a big hurry so that your prospective date will not have time to read the document. After getting the signature, your friend will leave the package, along with a carbon copy of the document, and depart. Upon opening the package your date will discover a note from you exhorting the reader to check the fine print of any document requiring a signature. Thus encouraged, your date will doubtless read the carbon copy and discover that a date has been agreed upon in writing.

Acknowledgement of Receipt

Name _____

Address _____

City _____ State ____ Zip _____

Shpmt _____ # of Cartons _____ Origin _____

I acknowledge receipt of the shipment described above. Undamaged carton(s) have been delivered by delivery person who will select person to date me, and I agree to and accept this date today.

_____/_____/_____
  Month   Day   Year

Signature _____

Working Late at the Office

This method takes the cooperation of your supervisor at work. Have your boss assign you and an associate a special project that needs to be completed immediately. The boss explains that the two of you must work late that evening on the project until it is done. Since it is going to be a long night, you are instructed to have dinner together before diving into the work. After the work is done, suggest that the two of you go out for coffee and dessert.

If the evening goes well, you may find yourself being requested to do special projects with your partner more often. Be sure to thank your supervisor for making you work late.

Try a Trick

This method is sly, underhanded, and dirty. But it works. The object is to trick the person into taking you out on a date—and paying for it, too.

To understand this one, listen to Stacy use the trick on Jim. Stacy first takes four one-dollar bills out of her wallet.

Stacy: I'll bet you I have five one-dollar bills right here.
Jim: It looks like you have four.
Stacy: No, I have five. Go ahead and look for yourself.
Jim: Four: one, two, three, four. There are only four.
Stacy: I say I have five.
Jim: You are crazy! There are only four.
Stacy: Okay. I say five; you say four. Will you buy my dinner if I'm wrong?
Jim: Sure. You are crazier than I thought, Stacy; there are only four: one, two, three, four. See four? Four.
Stacy: You will buy my dinner if I'm wrong?
Jim: Sure.
Stacy: Okay, I'm wrong. Where do you want to take me for dinner?

Jim was so concerned about the numbers that he neglected to listen carefully to what Stacy was really saying. (If you missed the trick, read through the dialogue again.)

Any amount of any object will work for a prop. If you know the key line and are confident when you say it, there is little chance of failure. Practice the dialogue on a friend until you know your lines, then go out and get a free meal.

Pop Quiz

Type up a quiz similar to the one shown here, and give it to the person you desire to date. Mail the quiz along with a stamped, self-addressed envelope.

Name _____
Today's Date _____

Quiz

Instructions: Please take this quiz and return it in the enclosed postage-paid envelope. Quizzes postmarked later than May 15 cannot be accepted.

1. Would you like to go on a picnic Saturday, May 25?
   ☐ a. Yes, but not with you.
   ☐ b. Yes, if I can bring my spouse.
   ☐ c. No, I hate finding ants in the potato salad.
   ☐ d. Yes, I would like that.
   ☐ e. Who are you?

If you checked d, proceed. If you checked a, b, c, or e, skip the remaining questions and return the quiz in the enclosed envelope.

2. There will be a jazz concert in the park; do you like jazz music?
   ☐ a. No, but I can bring earplugs.
   ☐ b. No, music makes me nauseous.
   ☐ c. Yes, but only on my home stereo—alone.
   ☐ d. Yes, but only in the park with you.
   ☐ e. Yes, but only when the band lets me play lead saxophone.

3. What time would you like me to pick you up?
   ☐ a. As late as possible. I don't want to miss Saturday morning cartoons.
   ☐ b. Don't bother—I'll hitchhike.
   ☐ c. 10:30 A.M.
   ☐ d. 11:00 A.M.
   ☐ e. 11:30 A.M.

4. About what time would you like to get home?
   ☐ a. At noon.
   ☐ b. Don't worry about it; when I get bored I'll just sneak away.

☐ c. About _____:_____ P.M.

☐ d. Only after you have treated me to a romantic and expensive dinner.

☐ e. Before my other date comes by to take me to dinner.

5. What do you plan on wearing?
   ☐ a. Something casual, in case I spill mustard all over me.
   ☐ b. Foul weather gear, in case the sprinklers come on.
   ☐ c. *Not* wedding attire. You certainly are pushy.
   ☐ d. An oxygen suit—I'm allergic to *everything*.

Still Shots

Take a series of self-portraits with a camera. In each shot, hold up a sign which displays a different word of a sentence like "Hello, would you like to go to the beach with me next Saturday?" To make things more fun, you can change your costume for each shot. Number each photograph, and deliver them individually to your prospective date over the course of two to three days. Leave the photos on the prospect's car windshield and desk at work, mail some, and have one delivered with flowers. With the last photo, include a self-addressed, stamped envelope and an instant camera. If your potential date is clever, you will receive an answer in living color.

Barter Dating

A roundabout way to ask someone for a date is to offer the person dinner in exchange for help in an area in which he or she is skilled. You can ask for assistance doing a school or office assignment, fixing your car, or filling out tax returns. The arrangement is mu-

tually beneficial: Your helper gets a free dinner and an opportunity to be helpful, and you receive help with a project and an evening with someone special.

Detective Shadowing

If the idea of posing as a detective appeals to you, try this fun way to ask someone out. To do a convincing job, you must use all the things you have learned from watching hundreds of detective shows on television.

Tell the person whom you wish to date that you are studying to become a private investigator and have been assigned the task of tailing someone for practice. Ask if the person would be willing to be followed for a day if you promise not to be bothersome. If the person agrees, select a day when you will do your assignment.

Arrive early in the morning, and leave a note on the person's car which says, "You are being watched." Write several similar notes beforehand so that you can leave them whenever your date-to-be runs into a store or leaves the car momentarily. If the person stops for lunch, find a way to pay the tab without being seen. Have the waitress explain, "The check was paid by a person who said you are being watched." Continue until the end of the day (or as long as you can), and then make your presence known by having a friend stage an attack* that you will fend off. After dealing with the attacker, hand the person a business card with your name and the name of a fictitious private investigations firm, along with the fees charged to clients: one hundred dollars per hour (three-hour minimum) or dinner Friday at seven. Even if the date is turned down, you can console your defeat with the hard-earned income.

One of the World's Worst Dates #3
March 23, 1985: Branson, Missouri

Rick Krueger went to Donna Gibson's farm for an afternoon of horseback riding. When Rick arrived, Donna had two of her horses saddled and ready for a ride. Since they had not dated much, Rick was still concerned about relating well to Donna. Therefore, when she asked if he knew how to ride, he answered, "Of course!"— even though he had never petted a horse, much less ridden one. After making a fool of himself trying to climb into the saddle, Rick endured nearly an hour of bone-jarring riding as he attempted to keep up with Donna. The afternoon's "fun" ended abruptly when Rick's horse— apparently tired of its pitiful load—halted suddenly in mid-gallop, sending Rick to the ground to receive a broken rib.

THE OUTCOME: The couple had one more date, but the roles were reversed as they rode motorcycles. Rick's rib healed nicely, but the back of Donna's favorite pair of jeans will never skid again.

---

*Be sure to do this when no one else is around. A stranger could witness your date-to-be's "plight" and take action. Aside from wanting to avoid possible violence, you don't want anyone else to steal your scene!

Small Talk

Here is a list of conversation-generating questions to help you and your date become better acquainted:

- What was the name of your favorite stuffed animal when you were little?
- Have you ever been to Wisconsin? (If you live there, answer yes.)
- What's your favorite ride at Disneyland or Disney World?
- What was your junior high school principal's name?
- Does your toilet tissue unroll from the top or from the back?
- If you could invent your own color, what would it look like?
- What do you think of Millie Schwartz's dish antenna?
- What is your mother's maiden name?
- Where did your ancestors come from? (Have you ever thought of returning there?)
- What would you do with one million dollars?
  What great authors do you read? (If they don't know any, suggest a few: Shakespeare, Sheldon, Hemingway, Fields, Temple, Dr. Seuss.)
- If you could live anyplace in the world, where would it be?
- Who was your favorite player with the 1969 Miracle Mets?
- If you were elected president, who would you appoint to your advisory council?
- Name every foreign country you have visited. (If you have not visited any, say Wisconsin.)

- Have you ever ridden a jet ski, snowmobile, hang glider, ATC, or camel?
- How do you feel about today's adiabatic lapse rate?
- What is your favorite flavor of ice cream?
- What is your favorite style of art?
- When you were little, what did you want to be when you grew up?
- What is your favorite food?
- If you were a bird, where would you fly (besides south)?
- What was your most embarrassing moment?
- Did you ever think of inventing something?
- What was the best gift you ever received?
- What was your best Christmas?
- What is your all-time favorite movie, song, or television show?
- How much do you weigh? (just kidding)
- If you could marry a movie star, who would it be?
- Have you ever eaten snails?
- What is your favorite bumper sticker?
- What is your favorite family tradition?
- Who was your childhood hero?
- What qualities do you look for in a friend?

Balloon Pop

Write this simple message on six different sheets of paper: "Will you go out with me?" Sign your name to each, then place the messages inside balloons before

MAKE CERTAIN YOUR PROSPECTIVE DATE HAS A VERY GOOD HEART.

inflating them. Place the balloons in your intended date's home or office so that the balloons will be popped when a door is opened or when a drawer is shut. When the balloons pop, your messages will be discovered by your prospective date. Provide an uninflated balloon into which the person can place the answer.

(This method is actually the contemporary form of an ancient practice which used pigeons to carry the messages. Because the birds were difficult to inflate and expensive to pop, balloons are now used.)

Selling Yourself

Corporate America spends billions of dollars on advertising each year, because advertising lets others know what the company has to offer. If you want to let a particular person know what a date with you has to offer, advertise.

Your promotional piece should communicate your desire to date the person and should include the details of the proposed date and the benefits of dating you. Look through magazines for material to construct an effective ad. Use headlines, catchy jingles, illustrations, and photographs to paste together a handbill or brochure. Mail the original artwork to your intended date, or print a copy on special paper using a high-quality photocopier. (If you use clippings of material protected by copyright or trade laws, print only one to avoid correspondence with corporate attorneys.) To test the effectiveness of your concept, always include a tear-off coupon that can be returned to you if the reader of the ad wants to strike a deal.

Should your initial advertisement prove effective, follow up with a complete campaign. Use a file to collect clippings and ideas which can be used later in a series of promotional pieces.

In addition to getting you a date, your clever ad may end up in your date's scrapbook as a reminder of the wonderful time you spent together. If your advertising concept is truly brilliant, you may consider opening an agency to handle the campaigns of friends.

Surveying the Situation

Hand a survey similar to this one to the person you wish to date. Explain that you are conducting a survey and would appreciate receiving the person's honest answers.

Survey

This survey is being conducted for statistical purposes. Please answer each question to the best of your ability.

1. *Sex:*   M ☐   F ☐
2. *Age:*   Under 18 ☐   Over 18 ☐
3. *Citizenship:*   US ☐   Other ☐
4. *Level of Education:*   High School ☐   College ☐ Graduate School ☐
5. *Occupation:* _____
6. *Marital Status:*   S ☐   M ☐   D ☐   Sep ☐   W ☐
7. Is English your primary language?   ☐ No   ☐ Yes
8. If you were asked on a date this week, where would you choose to go?
   ☐ canoeing
   ☐ dancing
   ☐ dinner
   ☐ jogging
   ☐ grunion hunting
   ☐ hang gliding
   ☐ on a picnic
   ☐ to Paris
   ☐ visit my Aunt Gertrude
   ☐ skateboarding
   ☐ to a drive-in
   ☐ other: _____

9. If you had a choice of how you would be picked up for a date, which means would you prefer?
   □ date's car
   □ limousine
   □ helicopter
   □ bicycle
   □ under the arms
   □ piggyback
   □ ambulance
   □ dog sled
   □ horse-drawn buggy
   □ other: _____

10. While on a date, how do you like to be treated?
    □ as a lady
    □ as a gentleman
    □ as a king
    □ as a queen
    □ as a parade float
    □ as a circus animal
    □ as a _____

11. If you were given an opportunity to go on a date with someone special this week, what day would you select?
    M □ Tu □ W □ Th □ F □ Sa □ Su □

12. If that date were to be with a certain survey conductor, would you accept? Yes □ No □

13. If, while on that date, this person tried to kiss you, what would you do?
    □ allow it
    □ pretend I didn't notice
    □ ask the person not to
    □ call for help
    □ punch the person out
    □ bite the person's lip
    □ other: _____

7.

The Art of Writing and Sending Notes

Notes are fun to give and to receive. They remind your special friend that he or she is on your mind. They also show how much you value the relationship since you are taking the time to do something extra.

If your special friend is leaving on a trip, send notes to where he or she is staying. Hide small notes inside your friend's luggage, briefcase, and pockets where they will be found later. Include small treats to make the discovery more fun.

If you are leaving on a trip, arrange to have your special friend receive a note each day you are gone; in this way you will be hard to forget. You will need an accomplice to help you mail or deliver notes so that each arrives on the correct day. If you are going on a fifteen-day trip, the following is an example of what your special friend could receive each day you are gone:

Day 1 A postcard
Day 2 A large musical eighth note cut out of black construction paper, left on the car windshield
Day 3 A letter
Day 4 A telegram
Day 5 A postcard sent to the office
Day 6 A small card inside car
Day 7 Helium balloons and a note tied to desk at work

Day   8 An electronically mailed note delivered to office
Day   9 A bouquet of flowers delivered to house
Day 10 A stuffed animal with a note left on door-step
Day 11 A UPS package delivered to office
Day 12 One rose in car with a note
Day 13 Two roses in car with a note
Day 14 Three roses in car with a note
Day 15 One dozen roses delivered personally when you return

To include this much variety in your note-sending, your accomplice will stay quite busy. Prepare a detailed list of tasks so that he or she will be able to deliver or mail each item at the proper time. Be sure to supply money, car key, and anything else needed to perform the surprises.

Another note-sending idea is to collect silly or bizarre postcards from other cities and countries as you travel. Save them in a file, occasionally selecting one at random to send to your friend. If you have family, friends, or associates who live in a distant country, ask them to send you a blank picture postcard. Write the postcard as if you were actually there, and address it to your special friend. Place it in an envelope, and mail it back to your distant connection with a note asking that the card be stamped and mailed for you. Depending on the postcard's arrival date, you may be able to convince your friend that you actually went to Sri Lanka or Tasmania the previous weekend.

When you want to send your friend a quick affirming or humorous note, a photocopier can help you print simple, yet creative, personal stationery. Find a word in the dictionary that describes this special person (e.g., "friend," "handsome," "beautiful," "special," "outstanding"); photocopy the word and its definition onto a piece of paper, and use the sheet as your stationery. If you find a headline, cartoon, or photograph that will bring joy or laughter to your friend, photocopy it. Write your note on the copy, and mail it. It is uncanny how a short, personalized note can bring your friend happiness after a long day.

If sending notes becomes a habit, you may soon tire of addressing each piece of mail the same way. To counteract this monotony, invent new ways to address correspondence. Try "Resident" or "Occupant." Use an "in care of" line to liven things up:

C/o Bizarre Postcards, Inc.
C/o The Millionaires' Club
C/o Dirk Nirdnik, Talent Agent
C/o Tom Selleck Look-alike Contest
C/o Acme Kissing School

The more personal you are, the funnier your "in care of's" will be.

Try including successively less information in your friend's address in a series of notes sent one day apart. (Be sure to put the return address on each letter.)

first letter:	include the entire address
second letter:	omit the city
third letter:	omit the city and street number
fourth letter:	include the city, omit the street number and name
fifth letter:	include only the name and zip
sixth letter:	include only the name

How fast the letters start returning will help you gauge just how well-known your special friend is.

When you have become a habitual note writer, you may wish to share some of your creativity with friends and encourage them to get hooked. There is also nothing wrong with sending fun notes to family members, friends, and associates who could certainly stand to have their days lightened by the discovery of a joyful note in the midst of sad bills and junk mail.

8.

Special Gifts from A to Z

Finding the perfect gift for a special friend is a constant problem for most of us. In this chapter, we have alphabetically listed seventy-eight unique gifts that your friend has possibly never before received. Under each letter, we have given you a choice of three gifts ranging from the affordable price of nothing to the outrageous price of everything you have and more.

- A -

Acre of Almonds. With the prices of almonds these days, this gift would be a worthwhile investment.

Affirmation. Giving this gift at every opportunity will change your special friend's life.

Airmail. Send letters and packages to your special friend by air, surface, electronic mail, pony express, or whatever.

- B -

Belief. Let your friend know you believe in him or her. You are who you are partly because someone believed in you.

Best Friend. Give your special friend an all-expenses-paid day with a best friend. Bring the friend in from out of town if need be, and supply the makings

127

for a memorable time together. This is an excellent way to show you care.

Box of Diamonds. A small box will most likely satisfy anyone. Make sure the gems are authentic and not merely glass imitations. If you are shopping in this category, you should know the difference.

- C -

Carriage Ride. You may have to look around for a horse-drawn carriage, but the trouble is worth it. Bring a blanket and something hot to drink while you take in the sights and enjoy the uniqueness of this gift.

Compliment. It is hard to put a price on a compliment. Take the time to notice the good in others. Mark Twain once said, "I can live two months on one compliment." So can others.

Cream-Colored Cadillac. This gift speaks—or rather shouts—for itself.

- D -

Daisy, Dianthus, Daffodil. If you can find the right garden, these gifts are free.

Delicatessen. This gift is just perfect for when your special friend gets hungry for a hot pastrami sandwich at three in the morning. (Make sure it is close to the house.)

Dessert. Prepare your friend's favorite. Since the person will not want to eat alone, make one for yourself too.

- E -

Everything. This gift is perfect for that hard-to-shop-for person.

Exotic Pet. This gift can range from a small fish, to a medium-sized gerbil, to a fat leopard.

HAPPY BIRTHDAY, CARL!
IT REMINDED ME OF YOU!

Extra Time and Effort. Because taking advantage of a special friend happens all too easily, try giving your friend some extra time and effort as often as possible.

- F -

Flower Shop. By buying the entire shop, you can avoid those last-minute trips to the florist for a rose.

Forgiveness. This gift may be free, but the one who is able to give it is wealthy indeed.

Frame a Favorite. Kidnap your friend's favorite poem, photo, or painting. Have it mounted in a frame.

- G -

Glass Blowing Lessons. Expect to receive plenty of blown glass gifts for a while.

Gloves. You may choose from a variety of gloves: driving, formal, golf, handball, ski, welding, motocross, lace, baseball, fur-lined.

Goals. Help the other person set goals. Set your own goals as to how you will treat the other person better. Also, set goals to spend quality play time together.

- H -

Hippopotamus. To save you trouble, pay the few dollars to have it gift-wrapped at the store.

Historical Relic. Some might call this an antique, but we were desperate for an "H." Give an old coin, a vintage photograph, or a well-aged book.

Hug. If you could package these, you would make a million dollars. Give this gift every day.

- I -

Inscription. Inscribe a significant message or quotation on something special.

Integrity. This trait can be a great gift when lived out in your actions.

Island. Buy a deserted tropical island. If cost is a factor, keep it small.

MY VERY OWN ISLAND! HOW SWEET!

...AND THERE'S A FIRECRACKER IN THE MIDDLE TO MAKE IT VOLCANIC!

- J -

Joke. With the right timing, this gift can improve anyone's attitude. (If the joke is good, of course.)

Journal. A journal for photos, quotations, or personal thoughts can be a good gift for someone who enjoys chronicling special moments.

Jungle. If you could not afford an island, a jungle is less expensive.

- K -

Kentucky Bluegrass. Buy as many acres as you can afford. If you are really wealthy, buy a Kentucky Derby winner—or even the state of Kentucky.

King. Treat the man in your life like a king. If you are a male looking for a special gift for the woman in your life, see "Q."

Knapsack. Prepare a knapsack filled with goodies for a picnic or as a care package for someone going away on a trip.

- L -

Leadership. Plan to do something with your special friend in which you take the initiative and lead. Do not

allow the other person to make any decisions. If you are normally the leader, switch roles and allow the other person to take charge for a while.

Letterhead Stationery. Design and have printed a set of personal stationery for a friend.

Library. Purchase a library and name it after your friend.

- M -

Marquee. Rent a theater or restaurant marquee, and display a personal message to your friend.

Mint. Not the breath type—the coin type.

Motivation. This gift helps others get excited about who they are and what they are doing.

- N -

Nonverbal Communication. Smiles, hugs, affirming touches, handshakes, and glances are great ways to communicate your feelings. Take advantage of this easy-to-use, silent gift.

Nourishment. Surprise your special friend in the middle of the day, late at night, or anytime with a fun treat. Frozen yogurt, a jar of nuts, a basket of fruit, or a glass of juice can give someone a much appreciated lift.

Nutmeg Farm. This gift is especially appreciated during the holidays.

- O -

Observation. Observe a unique quality in your special friend and comment on it.

Oneself. Have an accomplice deliver you (inside a box) to your special friend. Poke air holes in the box, and mark the outside "LIVE PLANT, OPEN IMMEDIATELY"—in case the recipient wants to wait until Christmas to open you.

Oyster Bed. This gift is ideal for the habitual pearl buyer. Be sure to hire divers.

- P -

Parking Lot. Purchase one for a person who has end-

Things NOT to Give as Gifts

This chapter provides a rather lengthy list of creative gifts from A to Z. A few items were purposely left off that list for obvious reasons. If you are inclined to give one of the items below—don't.

acne cream
bedpan
broken seashell
cemetery plot
Christmas ornament
   (in July)
clothing that is three
   sizes too large
dead animal
dead plant
deodorant insoles
egg timer
eight-track tape
exercise book
expired cottage cheese
exposed film
homemade sand
   candle

last year's calendar
lint remover
lunch with your
   newly divorced best
   friend
McDonald's gift
   ce⁻tificate
mirror that makes
   things seem larger
   than actual
mounted fish
mouthwash
old bowling trophy
old toothbrush
one-way ticket
   somewhere
personalized pencils
photo of your old

less trouble locating a parking space. If the lot is not conveniently located, hire a valet to do the parking.

Party. Throw a party for any reason: because he has blue shoes, because she has pretty eyes, because he fell while getting out of the car, or even because she lost her tennis tournament. The crazier the reason the more fun you may have.

Patience. Many people wish they had more of this quality. Try to use some around your special friend.

girlfriend or
  boyfriend
photos of a
  Harley-Davidson
  out of *Cycle News*
rubber snake
set of click-clacks

subscription to *The*
  National Enquirer
3–D glasses
toilet brush
tomcat
used cotton swab
weight reduction pills

- Q -

Quadriga. A two-wheeled Roman chariot drawn by four horses harnessed abreast. This gift may be a little difficult to get into your friend's living room.

YOUNG MAN, THAT QUADRIGA IS A VERY THOUGHTFUL GIFT, HOWEVER I'D LIKE YOU TO CLEAN UP AFTER IT.

Queen. Treat her like a queen—she deserves the best! She is a special person; treat her that way.

Quotation. Find a quotation that your special friend likes; have a calligrapher write it, and then frame it.

- R -

Relaxation. Dates can often be a source of stress. Let your date know ahead of time that you are looking forward to a relaxing time together. If you are the one planning the date, think ahead and provide a relaxing atmosphere. It will be an appreciated and refreshing gift.

Restore the Past. Locate a memento of your friend's past, and restore it as a gift. An old photograph, a childhood drawing, or an elementary school award will bring back favorite memories.

I'LL DRIVE, YOU JUST RELAX!

Reunion. Plan a reunion for your special friend. If second grade was a special year, arrange to have the person's entire second grade class flown in for the occasion.

- S -

Sacrifice. Go out of your way to put your special friend's desires and wants first. You may have to sacrifice your money, time, pleasure, or pride. Love equals commitment, and commitment requires sacrifice.

Stadium. This is a practical gift if your special friend is an avid sports fan. For an extra touch, purchase the home team.

Stamps. Assemble a "mailbox" for your friend. Include a roll of stamps, postcards, envelopes, a postage scale, and a rate schedule.

- T -

Tandem Bicycle. Rent, borrow, or buy one of these two-seaters, and take your friend on a wild ride.

Thankfulness. Count how many times you sincerely

say "thank you" in a day. Double that amount the next day. Write a letter listing everything you are thankful for in your special friend, and send it.

WELL, THANKS

Traffic Light. Does your date feel stress because of traffic (as most do)? Does traffic sometimes keep you from getting to your destination on time? If so, purchase a traffic light from your city, and make sure it is always green.

- U -

Umbrella. Do not buy just any umbrella; buy one that folds into an extremely small package, or has a radio in the handle, or doubles as a life raft in case of flood.

Ungulate Collection. While many well-to-do people pride themselves with a stable of horses, you can give that special friend a complete selection of hoofed animals including a tapir, a rhinoceros, and a couple of hyraxes.

Uplifting. Prepare a list of things that your special friend enjoys. Refer to that list when the person needs a lift.

- V -

Vacation. Treat your special friend to a long vacation. Pay the person a salary to take the entire year off.

Valentine. Why wait until February? Send valentine cards and gifts all year long; stock up on half-priced items at the sales following St. Valentine's Day.

Victory. Give your special friend the opportunity to be victorious in something. Encourage a new hobby; help with school studies; assist in the person's sports training.

- W -

Wild Berries. Locate a wild berry patch; pick a basket full, and present it to your friend. Bring along ice cream or pie fixings so the gift can be put to immediate use.

Wisdom. People are flattered when you ask for their opinions. Seek the wisdom of your special friend—and listen.

Woods. Many people own their own forests. Why should your special friend miss out on this privilege?

- X -

X. Giving a kiss is easy, inexpensive, and delightful.

Xebec. This three-masted Mediterranean sailing vessel makes a unique and much-talked-about gift, especially if anchored in your special friend's reflecting pool. Do not give to a xenophobe.

I UNDERSTAND THAT IT'S A SPECIAL GIFT, BUT SANDRA, YOU KNOW YOUR FATHER DOESN'T ALLOW ANY XEBECS IN THE REFLECTING POOL

Xerox. Make ten photocopies of your face, and mail, hide, post, and hand out the copies to your special friend. Your face will not be forgotten. Shut your eyes when copying to avoid becoming a blind date.

- Y -

Yankees. This gift is for someone who, as a kid, always got picked last when the teams were being chosen.

Yolk. Two egg yolks, some toast, and orange juice are perfect for breakfast in bed. You may want to add a little mouthwash to the orange juice just to be safe.

Youth. Allow your special friend to be young at heart. Encourage the childlike qualities that adults often lose, such as curiosity, innocence, pleasure in simple things, trust, and free-flowing laughter.

- Z -

Zany. Everyone needs to be zany once in a while. Skip down the street, practice talking like Donald

Duck, or face backward in a crowded elevator. "A merry heart makes a cheerful countenance, but by sorrow of the heart the spirit is broken" (Proverbs 15:13). Pass the gift of merriment on to your date.

Zeppelin. This rare gift is a romantic way to fly, especially if there is no hurry.

Zodiac. Rent one of these exciting inflatable boats, and take your special friend on an expedition around a lake or harbor. Bring a pump and patch kit. Do not wear golf shoes.

9.

Home Dates

Sometimes weather, circumstance, or just the desire to be indoors gives you the opportunity to date at home. This chapter is a collection of dating ideas designed to give you enough to do without even considering the dull and noncreative pastime known as watching television.

Battleship

Here's a game that doesn't involve much actual playing time but requires plenty of time during the preliminary construction period. The object of this game is to make battleships out of ordinary paper. Construct these ships in front of one another; decorate, name, and then christen them. Now make your way to the bathroom, and place them in the toilet. You may wish to add food coloring to the water to give it a deep blue look. Once your ships are afloat, wad up tissue-paper projectiles, and launch them with plastic spoon catapults. If the battle drags on too long, flush the toilet and watch the ships fight the storm. The last

ship to sink is considered the victor. Once the ships have sunk, make paper airplanes and have a dogfight.

Cookie Marathon

Use your kitchen as the seedbed of this idea. Get some aprons, make some chefs' hats, and prepare to spend the next few hours making several different types of cookies.

Make these cookies for your neighbors, your relatives, the residents of a nearby rest home, the church youth group, the gas station attendant, or anyone. While baking, take frequent instant pictures of yourselves, and give one of the photographs to a friend with a dozen cookies. Record a message to a friend living far away who will be delighted to listen to the tape, eat the cookies, and be reminded of the good friends back home. When a Girl Scout comes to your house to sell cookies, say no and give her a dozen instead. Go around town and give them away to people walking or working, or even give some to the policeman who pulls you over. All the effort is worth it to see the expression on their faces. Have fun with this one, sweet tooth.

Crawling Olympics

This home date may be a little tough on the knees, but it is lots of fun. Invent several sporting events that can be played by crawling about on hands and knees. Here are some ideas for your crawling olympics:

- *Loopathon:* See how many times each of you can loop around the house in one minute.
- *Dash:* Pick two spots in the house, and time yourselves racing from one spot to the next.
- *Hurdles:* These can be made by putting a broomstick across two glasses. Give penalty points for knocking down the broomstick.
- *Steeplechase:* This race goes up the stairs, over a couch, under a table, back down the stairs, out the front door, and ends with a somersault on the front lawn. Additional furniture can be added to make the course more difficult.
- *Relay Race:* This race works well if you have company over.
- *Figure-eight:* Set two chairs in the middle of the

room and form a figure-eight race track around them. Flip a coin for pole position, have pit stops, and get a soft drink company to sponsor your race.

- *Debris Race:* This race works best when you are house-sitting. Spend a few minutes before the race, and turn over all the furniture to create a huge mess. Now race around the house, and see who best manages the traffic jams.

- *Marathon:* Purchase a crawling odometer, and put it on your right leg; crawl around the house until you both reach twenty-six miles.

We hope these ideas will spur on your creativity, and allow you to have a wonderful date on your knees. Some helpful hints: (a) dresses don't make very good track suits; (b) if you live in an upstairs apartment, make sure the neighbors beneath you are out for the evening.

Food Swapping

If your date lives with roommates or family who aren't home at the moment, try this fun activity. Go into the kitchen, and proceed to swap food from one container to another. Put salt in the sugar bowl, cream in the milk carton, pepper in the salt shaker, potato chips in the cornflakes box, grapes and nuts in the cereal box, Ping-Pong balls in the egg carton, jello in the sour cream container, and so on.

The fun of this activity is long-lasting because you will get to hear the stories of how each swap was discovered and how revenge was taken on your date.

Money Scramble

When a lack of funds leaves you and your date at home with nothing to do, go on a treasure hunt. Go

FORTY-TWO CENTS!

YIPPEE!

through couches, love seats, and overstuffed chairs in search of coins and jewelry that have slipped between the cushions to hide amongst the ancient jelly beans, antique combs, and petrified potato chips. If your excavation produces funds insufficient for even a single scoop of ice cream, explore the dark recesses of your car seats.

Hide and Seek

This date is a slightly modified version of the timeless childhood classic. One person waits outside the front door while the other person finds a place within the house to hide. After two minutes have passed, the seeker comes in the house and shouts one of the following phrases:

- "Here I come, ready or not" (West Coast).
- "I'll find you quicker than a cat finds a leaky cow" (Midwest).

- "This is the police, come out with your hands up" (big cities).
- "Time's up, here I come" (everyone else).

As soon as the warning is shouted, the seeker searches the house to find the person hiding in the least possible time. Take turns, and time each other until you run out of places to hide or one of you gets lost.

Hide and Scare

This date is a variation of "Hide and Seek" that includes more anxiety and laughter. The rules are similar to the traditional version, except that all the lights are turned off in the house. The object of the game is for the seeker to find the person hiding before the hider jumps out and scares the seeker. If the seeker finds the hider first, you simply switch roles; but if the hider is able to jump out and scare the seeker, the hider receives scare points.

Scare points are awarded as follows:

Seeker's reaction	Points
none	0
silent flinch*	100
gasp** and flinch	200
jump	300
scream	400
jump out window	disqualified
faint***	1000

... AND HE WAS DEARLY LOVED BY ALL HIS FRIENDS, EXCEPT SALLY WHO SCARED HIM TO DEATH.

WARNING: This game is not to be played underwater, in the presence of large, hungry animals, or by those who are pregnant, have heart conditions, or are emotionally unstable.

*A sudden and involuntary muscular reaction.
**An abrupt and audible inhalation or exhalation.
***A temporary loss of consciousness usually causing collapse.

Carob Date (Brownies)

2 cups chopped dates
1 cup boiling water
1 teaspoon salt
2 heaping teaspoons
   baking soda
1 cup honey
1 cup flour

4 eggs beaten
2 tablespoons carob
   powder
1 cup carob chips
1 ½ cups chopped
   nuts

Preheat oven to 400°. Add dates and salt to boiling water, and let sit covered while mixing all other ingredients. Beat the eggs and add honey. Mix dry ingredients together, and blend with egg mixture. Fold in dates with water, along with carob powder, and mix well. Bake in 9″ x 13″ pan for 25–30 minutes or in muffin pan for 20 minutes. This recipe may never work, but it sure sounds good.

Household Math

The overwhelming concensus among accountants surveyed* is that "Household Math" is the best home date they have ever experienced. Grab your calculator and note pad—the "bottom line" of this date is worth it.

Wander through the house making the following calculations:

1. Count the number of windows.
2. Multiply this amount by the number of doorknobs.

---

*Doug's father was the only person who returned the survey.

3. Divide by the number of sinks.
4. Subtract the number of dirty dishes.
5. Add the number of home-care products in the showers.
6. Multiply this amount by the number of clocks.
7. Divide by the number of items stuck to the refrigerator.
8. Subtract the number of pairs of shoes in the closet.

After completing the above calculations, visit your date's home and follow the same formula. Compare the results: high number cooks dinner; low number cleans up.

Board Games

Board games do not have to be "bored" games. Mix several games together, and create new rules. Let the person whose turn is next make up new rules that will be advantageous to him or her. Set an egg timer to go off every three minutes, signaling you to switch places around the board. Do whatever you want; remember that the real object of the game is to make you laugh and to put a smile on your face.

Furniture Walk

The object of this game is to get from the front door to the back door without ever touching the floor. If you have an apartment with only one door, try to get through every room in the same manner.

With careful planning and catlike moves, you can bounce or walk across couches, swing upon doors, creep with rocking chairs, and ride tea carts in your aerial trek. Take turns until one of you is victorious, then compete for time. If one of you is a gymnast, even things out by completing the task backward, blindfolded, or balancing a tray with a china tea service in one hand.

YOU LOSE.

Surprise Hunt

In preparation for this date, you will need to write a series of clues that will lead your date on a hunt

through your house in search of special surprises.
Here is an example:

When your date arrives for dinner, she finds clue
number one pinned to the front door.

Welcome, my friend, I'm glad you are here.
I waited all day for this time to draw near.
Now that you've come, proceed to the room
Where people cook and I keep the broom.
Your first gift is there, and it's not a mink,
But make sure you look in the kitchen __ __ __ __.

When she looks in the sink, she will find a rose with
the next clue attached. It reads:

I'm glad you saw past the sponge
and found the rose.
The next clue swims in the room
where you blow your nose.

She will find floating in the tub a watertight lidded
bowl containing a favorite cassette tape and the third
clue.

I thought you would enjoy our favorite sounds; put
this tape in the player, and search for the next clue
with your ears. I hope you can bear this game
we're playing.

"CLUE # 26: PROCEED IN AN EASTERLY DIRECTION COUNTING OUT FOUR THOUSAND SIX HUNDRED EIGHTY-TWO STEPS, THEN TURN RIGHT."

You guessed it; on the stereo speaker she discovers a stuffed teddy bear holding the next clue.

You're in control in this date. Give as few or as many clues as you want. Your clues need not be brilliant (these certainly aren't). Your surprises can include gifts, flowers, or even portions of the meal. The greatest gift your date will receive is knowing that you gave so much time and effort to make him or her feel special.

10.

Creating Your Own Special Date

Creating a personal and innovative date is one of the best ways you can demonstrate to a special friend that you care. The time, effort, and love you put into producing a memorable experience all declare the value you place in the relationship.

To understand how to create a special date, you need to look at why one dates at all. A date is time spent exclusively with another person for your mutual enjoyment and the building of a relationship. In order for healthy relationships to grow and be maintained, you must spend significant amounts of quality time together so that you can get to know each other.

When preparing to date someone, ask yourself two questions. First, do I want to make this person feel special by providing an enjoyable experience? Second, do I want to spend time in the hope of establishing or maintaining a relationship with this person? If your answer to both of these questions is yes, this person is worth spending the time to please.

There are other reasons for dating, yet most of these stem from selfish motives. If you are dating to impress, show off, earn favors, pretend to be someone you are not, or control another person's schedule, your dates will lack the most important ingredient: putting your date first.

Make It Personal

When the relationship is very special (or you hope that it will be), it is only fitting that you make your time together very special. If your first desire is to make the experience completely enjoyable for your special friend, you will need to know what pleases him or her.

Be observant when the two of you are together; make a point of searching for clues to likes and dislikes. Ask questions. If you discover that your friend is fond of classical music, make arrangements to attend a concert. If noisy, crowded places are on the list of least favorites, stay away from motorcycle races, night-clubs, and roller derbies. Make a file of your date's likes and dislikes using the following list. Include some of these favorites in the date to make it personal:

Favorite colors:
Favorite type of music:
Favorite travel destinations:
Favorite foods:
Favorite desserts:
Favorite influential people:
Favorite hobbies:
Favorite flowers:
Favorite sports/pastimes:
Favorite fantasies:
Favorite personality likes/dislikes:
Other special interests:
Favorite toothpaste:
Favorite perfume/cologne:
Best friends:
Favorite books:
Favorite cartoon character:
Dream car:

Clothing styles:
  sizes:
Favorite animals:
Favorite drinks:
Favorite retreat spots:
Where he/she parks:
Favorite restaurants:
Work schedule:

The following date is an example of how the file can be used to make a simple date personally enjoyable for your special friend.

When you pick up your date, give her a gardenia cor-

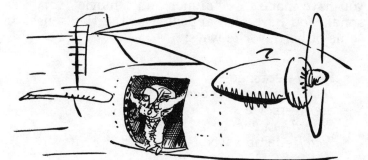

THIS IS A GREAT IDEA FOR A DATE, RON!

sage (her favorite flower). Go to dinner at her favorite Japanese restaurant. Afterward, see an old Barbra Streisand (her favorite singer) movie at the inexpensive theater that only shows reruns. When the show is over, drive to an all-night market and pick up some vanilla ice cream and chocolate chip cookies (her favorite dessert). Eat these in the car by dipping the cookies in the ice cream. Play a new Streisand album (which you will give to her) on the stereo. When the chill of the ice cream begins to take effect, present her with the lamb's wool scarf you saw her eye once when shopping (one of her favorite materials).

Through careful planning and proper use of the file, you have made this "dinner and a movie" very personal. You have also appealed to the five senses in some of her favorite ways:

- *Smell*—corsage
- *Taste*—dinner and dessert
- *Sight*—movie
- *Sound*—music
- *Touch*—lamb's wool

By making the effort to include things that your friend feels are special, you communicate that you listen carefully and that you think he or she is important enough to go out of your way to make happy.

Make It Memorable

The above date used a technique that not only makes the date more personal, but more memorable. Since all five senses were appealed to during the event, there is a great likelihood that the date is permanently embedded in your friend's memory. By including various sensory experiences in your date, you will heighten the enjoyment now and provide fond memories later on.

Another way to make a date memorable is to capture moments of it on film. So long as the picture-taking does not dominate the event, the photographs taken can be important reminders of enjoyable times spent together.

A third method to use when creating a memorable date is to include a new experience in the schedule. If your date experiments with a new activity during the event, that moment will be the basis of comparison for all subsequent experiences. For example, introduce your date to shaved ice, rock climbing, white grape juice, puddle jumping, helicopters, or bluegrass music. Even if your date decides never to experience the activity again, you will nonetheless have made the moment quite memorable.

Make It Unique

When designing your own creative date, one of the greatest sources for inspiration is other people's ideas. There is a temptation to want to use original ideas exclusively, but giving in to this temptation will only limit the possibilities for potential winners. No doubt, most of the dates in this book have been tried by couples before. What makes a date unique is the personal way in which you combine many different ideas. The ideas in this book can be one source for material. Another good source is friends who share your desire to make their dates feel special. Swap your best ideas, and brainstorm on new variations. In fact, if you have any date ideas that you would like to share, send them our way.

Make It Flexible

Special moments in a relationship are often unscheduled. Your best plans will be subject to the attacks of weather, traffic, mechanical breakdowns, and anything else that can possibly work against you. Remember that if your desire is to give your date an enjoyable time and to grow in your relationship, even mistakes, mishaps, and minor disasters can be used in your favor.

First, include an alternate plan. What will you do if it's raining the day of your picnic or cloudy the day you are going to the beach? Plan B could well end up being the best day the two of you have spent together.

Second, realize that occasionally something will happen that was unavoidable. A dress torn in a car door, a flat tire, a cherry pie in the lap, a sprained an-

DON'T BE SO HARD ON YOURSELF.
YOU THOUGHT YOU WERE GIVING THE
OFFICER'S WIFE A COMPLIMENT, WHEN
YOU TRIED OUT YOUR SPANISH.

kle on the dance floor, a sold-out show—these things will take place despite your best efforts. The interesting thing is that at such times as these you and your date get to see one another far more realistically. Anyone can be pleasant when things go smoothly; it is how a person acts when things turn bumpy that is the true character test.

Make It a Surprise

Most people are pleased by a surprise. They are flattered to know that they were the reason for much careful planning, secrecy, and effort. Surprises also serve to remind others that you as instigator are slightly unpredictable and mysterious.

There are many types of surprises, including those that frighten, shock, disappoint, or embarrass. In planning a surprise, avoid these kinds and concentrate on the types that amaze, please, or excite. To make your surprises effective, ask yourself, "What are the most delightfully unexpected things I could do for my special friend?" Write a list of all the answers that come to mind, no matter how preposterous. Now go back through the list, select an item that would be possible now, and make plans to include it in your date.

A note of caution is in order at this point. Before planning an elaborate surprise that involves a great deal of time, money, or effort, first be certain that your date enjoys surprises. Some people have a difficult time enjoying an evening so filled with surprises that they do not know what is going to happen next. Try a few small surprises to test your date's reactions before trying anything elaborate.

Make It Comfortable

When designing a special date, carefully consider the kind of atmosphere you wish to create. Take into account your date's personal schedule; will your friend desire an exciting release from a monotonous task, or a relaxing retreat from a highly pressured week? If you are unfamiliar with the atmosphere of a restaurant or other planned destination, check it out beforehand. A restaurant quiet on weekdays may have live rock bands on the weekend, and a very lively night spot may be closed on certain days.

Since the atmosphere of a setting is the product of all the sights, sounds, smells, tastes, and textures experienced in it, it is possible to create or enhance a romantic atmosphere by adding a few small touches. Here are some of the most obvious:

- Flickering candles
- Crackling fire
- Soft music
- Sparkling liquid refreshment
- Crystal stemware
- Soft chairs

Each person has a number of things that he or she finds romantic, and including some of these items will help you create the desired atmosphere.

Make It Consistent

Your creativity is an important extension of yourself. If you place great value in your and your date's relationship, place a corresponding amount of effort into the way you demonstrate that value. If this person is important in your life, share that fact by committing yourself to his or her happiness. When all is said and done, the date that is the most personal, memorable, and unique is the date that you create from your heart.

YOUR DATE IDEA COULD BE WORTH $500

Do you have a good date idea that you would like to share with others? Send your brainstorm to us. If we publish it in a future book we will send you $10.00 and print your name with your contribution. If we select yours as the most creative idea in the book, you will get a check for $500.00!

Don't keep your creative date to yourself. Write it down and send it to us with this form. Be sure to explain the idea as clearly as possible.

FILL OUT:

NAME _____

ADDRESS _____

CITY_____ STATE_____ ZIP_____

I hereby submit the attached dating idea(s) for possible publication in a future book on creative dating, attesting that to my knowledge the publication of these ideas by the authors of Creative Dating does not violate any copyright belonging to another party. I also understand that I will receive payment for these ideas if published by the authors, the amount to be determined by the authors, payable upon publication.

SIGNATURE_____ DATE_____

Write out or type your dating idea(s) and attach it to this form. Put your name somewhere on the idea(s) as well. Submitted material cannot be returned. Send to:

**CREATIVE DATING
P.O. BOX 8329
NEWPORT BEACH, CA 92658–8329**